# Powerhouse Business Mentorship

# Powerhouse Business Mentorship

*A How-To Handbook for Mentors and Mentees*

Jay J. Silverberg

**BEP**
BUSINESS EXPERT PRESS
Leader in applied, concise business books

*Powerhouse Business Mentorship:*
*A How-To Handbook for Mentors and Mentees*

Copyright © Business Expert Press, LLC, 2025

Cover design by Charlene Kronstedt

Interior design by Exeter Premedia Services Private Ltd., Chennai, India

First published in 2024 by
Business Expert Press, LLC
222 East 46th Street, New York, NY 10017
www.businessexpertpress.com

ISBN-13: 978-1-63742-702-6 (paperback)
ISBN-13: 978-1-63742-703-3 (e-book)

Business Expert Press Entrepreneurship and Small Business
Management Collection

First edition: 2024

10 9 8 7 6 5 4 3 2 1

*You cannot teach a man anything. You can only help him discover it within himself.*

—Galileo Galilei (1564—1642)

*This is my fifth book in the business series, and it has given me a unique perspective of the entrepreneurship arena. It can be a tough slog, but there is help. It's called mentoring, or mentorship.*

*Business is not easy but, as entrepreneurs, we make it more difficult by assuming too much, and wanting heaps of prosperity and breakneck success, all on our terms.*

*When we recognize the laws of the universe, that the world owes us nothing, that is when our true entrepreneurial butterfly bursts out of the "give me, I deserve it" cocoon.*

*Nothing good, I mean really good, happens overnight. Business takes time. The pathway to success is cratered with challenges we have to overcome, and quagmires that try to swallow us. But we survive.*

**Mentorship can make all the difference to us. It is our resource, safety net, sounding board, and trusted confidante who has our best interests at heart.**

*This book is dedicated to the countless personal and professional mentors who took me under their wing, listened to my ideas without chuckling, calmed me down when I worked myself up, and never, ever said "No, you can't do it."*

*"Thank you" is not nearly enough.*

*Now it's my turn to give back.*

*And to all the mentees who may embark on their own entrepreneurial mentorship journey, this handbook is for you. It will make your odyssey easier.*

*Finally, to my wife, Linda, my patient sounding board, gentle critic, and full-time inspiration, thank you for listening and being there.*

# Description

*Powerhouse Business Mentorship* **is the Definitive Business/Entrepreneurial Mentoring Handbook.**

Mentoring embraces vision-building, handholding, numbers-crunching, and encouragement. It's a two-way street consisting of the **mentor** (advisor/coach) and the **mentee** (the committed participant).

For the **mentor**, *Powerhouse Business Mentorship* offers powerful, success-oriented techniques and proven strategies that can assure a mutually effective mentorship experience. For the **mentee**, this book counsels on how to choose a mentor, how to control the process, and how to get the most out of the relationship.

Mentoring is not all about "You need to do it this way, my way," but more so, "Tell me what you are trying to do and where you want this opportunity to take you."

*Powerhouse Business Mentorship* also recounts Jay's mentoring journeys. Some were great and delivered memorable outcomes, some merely good, and others best described as … "colorful."

Everything Jay has learned from his mentoring encounters has found its way into *Powerhouse Business Mentorship*.

**Anyone leading or participating in mentorship needs to have** *Powerhouse Business Mentorship* **as their indispensable handbook.**

## Keywords

mentoring for entrepreneurs; finding a business mentor; mentorship gameplanning; mentee readiness; tools for successful mentors; tips for successful mentors; advice for business mentors; mentorship as a journey; business mentorship templates; business models for consultants; mentorship readiness test; business models for mentors and mentees; mentee guidelines; how to mentor; how to be an effective mentee; steps to successful mentoring; building the mentor-mentee relationship; elements of mentoring; toxic business mentoring; manual for mentors; guide to mentoring; skills of successful mentors; choosing who to mentor; the role of mentees; when mentoring succeeds; measuring mentoring success; when mentoring fails; choosing mentees; business mentoring framework; practical guide to mentoring; business mentor's toolkit; proven approaches for mentoring; principles of business mentoring; how to be a successful business mentor; mastering business mentoring

# Contents

# Testimonials

"Powerhouse Business Mentorship *is a must for anyone about to enter or is already in a mentor/mentee relationship. Practical advice on finding the right fit, how to work together and manage expectations, all based on real-world situations.* **Mentors would be well advised to give their mentees a copy of this book at the very first meeting. Sooner if possible.**" —**Lex Dunn, President, Encore Coaching**

"*As always, Silverberg's message is timeless, effortless and profound.* With so much experience under his belt, it is clear he has waded through the river from one side to the other and back again. The personal anecdotes, written with wonderful relatedness and joviality, add to what is at once a very important guide to mentors and mentees alike but also a novel of life experience. **Silverberg lays out the book in detailed measures whereby you may flip to the section that best resonates for you to get what you need, or alternatively you can read it from the beginning to the end to absorb all the sage wisdom.** Information is distilled in a concise and easy to read format resulting in a guide, which, although detailed, flows swiftly. Silverberg's wry wit peppered throughout and his way with the English language makes this a pleasure to read." —**Sara-Jane Brocklehurst, J.O.A.T. Consulting**

"*I have thoroughly enjoyed* Powerhouse Business Mentorship. *The book opened my eyes to implementable processes I can introduce to my staff.* **After reading Powerhouse Business Mentorship, I have decided to use the book's strategies and ideas to motivate our staff and increase their productivity.**" —**Michael Colclough, Executive Director, The Wachiay Group Inc., CEO, Wachiay Studio Inc.**

"*This book is a must read not only for those wishing to start a business, but also for those already in business.* **The invaluable advice Jay offers can be a game changer that delivers sustainable mentoring results.** *Congrats to Jay for* *sharing his many years experience with all who will take the time to wisely use this book as a guide.* **I'm sure that this** Powerhouse Business Mentorship **handbook** *will be a most welcome addition to and compliment with his entire business book collections.*" —Leslie Zietsman, Managing Director, Bourne Brothers Insurance

"*Mr. Silverberg has crafted a clear pathway to the art of mentoring.* **Powerhouse Mentorship** *is a great addition to the 'how to' knowledge base. His style ties together the steps to real-life mentoring activities and provides examples of both successes and failures.* **There is plenty for the beginner to digest, and an awesome review for the seasoned mentor.**" —James V Schneider, President, JV Schneider & Associates

"*As the former CEO of a financial services company, I experienced the power of mentoring in advancing corporate goals.* **Powerhouse Business Mentorship** *is a no nonsense and realistic read from Jay Silverberg, a veteran mentor,* who has obviously lived in the business trenches. Real accomplishment in the business world isn't about what might be; it's about achieving your goals, and that's the soul of this book." —Bruce E. McLean, Business Author

"*Jay has put into* Powerhouse Business Mentorship *all the strategies that helped our organization succeed in mentoring a new generation of community leaders.*" —Cristina Armstrong, Executive Director/Founder, Stewards of Sc'ianew Society Inc.

# Prologue

## Nepotism Can Be Messy

*We're here for a reason. I believe a bit of the reason is to throw little torches out to lead people through the dark.*

—Whoopi Goldberg

Burton spearheaded a very successful commercial chemical manufacturing business, one handed down to him by his father, who inherited it from his brother, who, in turn …. Well, I think you get it. The business had a long and illustrious family lifeline.

It was one of those low-key businesses that few ever heard of, but still managed to realize a respectable profit every year for the last seventy-five years. That is, until now.

Burton was of the age where, to him, retirement meant starting work at 7 AM instead of 5. Work ethic was part of his "old school" DNA. Always had been since he started as a chemical vat cleaner in the plant, the absolutely worst job his father could find for him. It was part of his training, and he wore his experiences well as he advanced years later to running and owning the company.

Yet the dirt under his permanently stained fingernails was an image that stayed with him. It was the yardstick by which he expected to measure his son, daughter, son-in-law, daughter-in-law, and his first wife who were all employed by and generously compensated by the firm.

The joke silently and mischievously circulated by the company's nonfamily management was that for every five thousand gallons of toilet cleaner that was sold, someone in the family bought a scandalously expensive car. Nothing pedestrian, you understand. It was a competition that rewrote the definition of entitlement, and it adversely impacted everybody (nonfamily) else's desire, loyalty to the firm, and motivation. The company's downward spiral slithered unabated.

But none of this was evident to me at the time when Burton called me in for a consult. We had met years back at a conference, formed an intuitive bond, and stayed in touch ever since.

"The last couple of years have not been kind." There was a distinct air of sorrow and anguish in his confession. "We're actually barely breaking even. That's never happened before. Ever!"

"And it's because … ?" I countered, hoping for some greater insight.

"I think it's because of my family. Honestly, I kind of expected little of them, and am getting even less than that. I think my family working here is too fat and happy, and need some coaching to do their jobs better. Or, just to do their jobs!" He ended with a sad chuckle.

I arranged a family workshop on defining responsibilities, setting performance targets and each of them taking ownership of their uber-scarce successes as well as their abundant shortcomings. It turned into a "bitch-slapping" session, each accusing the others, but accepting no responsibility for their own lackluster performance.

As weeks went by and I peeled back the layers of rampant nepotism, I was astonished at the detached and disinterested attitude of Burton's clan.

It reminded me of an oft-quoted Arabian proverb.

*My grandfather rode a camel, my father rode a camel, I ride a Mercedes, my son rides a Land Rover, and my grandson is going to ride a Land Rover, but my great-grandson is going to have to ride a camel again.*

*"Why is that?" he was asked. And his reply was—"Hard times create strong men. Strong men create easy times. Easy times create weak men. Weak men create difficult times. Many will not understand it but you have to raise warriors, not parasites."*

Competition among the family was primarily outside of business; jostling for position as their great-grandmother was terminally ill and was rumored to be rewriting her will. Entitlement 101.

Everyone facetiously called the daughter "Princess Prima Donna," a title she actually relished, completely missing the not-so-subtle contempt. She also thought that her role of VP Marketing required simply whirling into (and quickly out of) the office in ever-pricier outfits, to the utter dismay of her marketing staff.

The son rarely made an appearance. He traveled abroad extensively, apparently shopping for new product licensing opportunities and acquisitions, as was his responsibility. In five years, he brought painfully little to Burton, other than (and you can't make this stuff up) a line of disposable Caribbean scrub brushes.

My recommendation to Burton was simple.

"No offense, but you have spoiled your kids. But you know that. Your other family relations here are no better. I have tried to mentor them and explain what is expected of them, but their attention spans are barely childlike."

"If you want to retire, you need to fire them all, replace them with new blood, offer profit-sharing or stock option plans, and let the newbies recapture your business's greatness. You want out. I understand that. But you won't really be able to sell the company and retire with these lemmings in tow."

It was a bitter pill for Burton, but he agreed.

I brought in a Career Development Coach to help the now dislodged family of parasites, but, predictably, not one of them ever booked a meeting with the lonely mentor.

The transition took about eighteen months once the blood-letting was done. It worked. By then, I was very familiar with the business and spent time mentoring the newly hired team.

Burton also became my mentee. At that level, a "mentor" becomes an "advisor" or "counsel." Same thing, though, just a fancier title and higher fees.

I worked with him to package and value his business, to identify who the most cash-rich potential buyers were, and how to attract them to the negotiating table. Two years later, Burton sold his business.

Today, he lives in his villa on the Turks and Caicos Islands. His unemployed children will not talk to him, and that is just fine by him. He is content. He knows they will be back for the reading of his Will, which he hopes is many years away. He quips "There will be surprises."

I am hoping to attend, but not too soon.

# The Powerhouse Mentorship Handbook in a Nutshell

The following parallels the chapters, content, and information flow of this Powerhouse Mentorship Handbook. It provides the reader with an overall perspective of the full mentorship journey.

| | **CHAPTER 1—What Exactly Is Mentorship?** |
|---|---|
| The Mentoring Model | Graphic illustration of the entire integrated process of mentorship, start to finish, including anticipated deliverables and outcomes. |
| Mentorship Provides and Delivers | Highlights of what mentorship provides the stakeholders and what quantifiable results can be achieved. |
| Why Mentorship Succeeds | Statistical data on the success of mentorship as well as the reasons it works. |
| Why Mentorship Fails | Examining the downside of mentorship and identifying the factors that contribute to a failure of the process. |
| The Mentorship Scorecard | Use of a proprietary "scorecard" to track the mentorship journey, and examples of three scenarios tracking mentoring campaigns (good, bad, and ugly) using the scorecard model. |
| The Origin of the "Mentor" | Brief discussion on the origin of mentoring, and why mentorship has remained a mainstay for conveying information and sharing experiences. |
| Mentoring Adventures and Misadventures | Scattered throughout this book are "adventures and misadventures" real-life case studies, including the lessons drawn from these experiences. |
| | **CHAPTER 2—The Mentor** |
| Are you Mentoring Material? | Take the "Mentoring Skills Test" and identify your mentoring strengths, weaknesses, and possible gaps. |

| | |
|---|---|
| Defining Your Core Skills | "Core skills" go beyond helping others. They reflect the inherent abilities and personality needed to be an effective mentor. How do you rate? The following essential qualities are discussed.<br>• *The Two-Way Relationship*<br>• *Being on the Same Wavelength*<br>• *Parent-to-Adult Connection*<br>• *Be an Attentive Listener*<br>• *Understanding Expectations*<br>• *Devoting Your Time*<br>• *Building Mutual Trust*<br>• *Knowing When to Give Advice*<br>• *Being a Resource for the Mentee*<br>• *Always Showing Engagement*<br>• *Focus, Focus, Focus*<br>• *Understanding Your Own Limitations*<br>• *The Mentor as the Instructor*<br>• *Two-Way Feedback*<br>• *Parenting and Risk-Adversity*<br>• *The Mentor as the Networker/Connector*<br>• *Roots Mentoring*<br>• *Using Humor in Mentoring*<br>• *Looking After the Mentee's Best Interests* |
| Mentoring Etiquette: Code of Conduct for Mentors | What mentors need to build into any effective mentorship experience; starting with valuing and respecting the mentee. |
| The Rewards of Mentorship for the Mentor | What do mentors get out of the mentoring process? What rewards do they reap? Satisfaction? Yes. Becoming a better communicator and leader? Yes. The mentor learns as well as teaches. This chapter highlights the major benefits, most of which are qualitative in nature. |
| What Mentors Should Not Do | The mentorship process can go sideways; exceeding boundaries, leading instead of listening, or treating mentees as free labor. These are mentorship-slayers. |
| Mentoring Adventures and Misadventures | Protecting the mentee: An example when the mentor needed to raise a red flag and cry out "danger." |
| | **CHAPTER 3—The Mentee** |
| Defining the Types of Mentees | From the cautious and suspicious participants to the zealots looking for instant gratification, mentees vary dramatically. As a mentorship prerequisite, mentors need to recognize and understand who they are dealing with, and what they have signed up for. |
| The Mentee is the Flip Side of the Mentoring Process | Mentorship demands that the mentor needs to start "getting their arms" around the mentee. Basic questions form the foundation of a "Core Screening Document" between the parties. |

| | |
|---|---|
| Are You Ready to Be a Mentee? Getting into a Mentee's Head | An "Entrepreneur Self-Assessment Checklist" helps the mentee recognize their strengths, weaknesses, and possible threats circling their ideas. Further, the checklist gives the mentor the tools by which to establish a mentorship gameplan that builds on the mentee's recognition of their own abilities, vision, and needs. |
| What Mentees Should Do | Mentees have a responsibility to play by a series of rules and etiquette. These include having a clear vision of what they are looking for in a mentor and what they hope mentorship can achieve for them. |
| Beware the Toxic Mentor! | While this may sound like a "B" sci-fi movie, mentees can connect with a mentor who is not healthy for them; critical, self-absorbed, preachy, and other characteristics that harm rather than help the mentee. This chapter identifies the warning signs. Diligence is called for. |
| Mentoring Adventures and Misadventures | Depicts the author's personal mentoring experiences, each delivering a valuable lesson. |
| | **CHAPTER 4—Gameplanning the Mentorship Journey** |
| The Mentorship Relationship-Building Gameplan | This entire section is dedicated to the "how to" workings of the mentorship model. It starts with gameplanning—a series of well-defined stages directed toward realizing a viable mentorship journey for all parties. |
| Preliminary Meeting Online or Face-to-Face | This represents how the initial meeting between the parties can build familiarity and encourage the joint adoption of rules and guidelines that represent a workable, effective mentorship framework. |
| Agreement Between Both Parties | Building the relationship based on establishing both parties as equal players, recognizing the strengths of the mentor, and defining the needs of the mentee. Assuring that the matchup between the two is compatible is key. |
| The Core Screening Process | A critical component of gameplanning is determining the compatibility of styles and communication between mentor and mentee and identifying the relative contributions of each party. Further, this stage assesses the entrepreneurial strengths of the mentee and sets direction for the ensuing mentorship program. This "core screening" also includes a review of the "Self-Assessment Checklist" completed by the mentee. <br>• *Presenting the Entrepreneur's Self-Assessment* <br>• *Checklist* <br>• *Reviewing the Checklist Together* <br>• *Setting Needs and Expectations* <br>• *Defining the Mentor's Role* <br>• *The Crucial Reality Check* <br>• *Deep Diving* <br>• *Setting Achievable Milestones and Timelines* |

| Create a Mentorship Contract | One often-used strategy is to commit to paper the proposed mentorship arrangement. This defines each stakeholder's roles and responsibilities, jointly defines the anticipated goals and vision, and sets up the etiquette and guidelines each player is expected to follow. While this is a moral contract at best, the process of both the mentor and the mentee signing off on the contract, solidifies the workings of the mentorship journey (a *sample Mentorship Contract is included in this chapter*). |
|---|---|
| Time for a SWOT Analysis (Strengths, Weaknesses, Opportunities, Threats) | During the course of carrying out the mentorship journey, time needs to be set aside to compare what was originally planned versus what the process is realizing. This is a "work in process" stage. |
| Setting Mentoring Get-Togethers | An important component of gameplanning is agreeing upon a schedule of meetings (online, face-to-face) and tracking each participant's adherence to the schedule. |
| Role Playing | Often defined as theatrics, this mentoring tool allows the mentor to take on other roles, such as the funder. It provides a more real mentorship experience for the mentee. |
| The Funnel Effect | Funneling means keeping the process on track by prioritizing what topics are covered and dissuading any shifts away from key issues. This minimizes distraction and unproductive segways. |
| Storytelling | Learning by example is a strong component of mentoring, and generally provides the mentee with concrete lessons relating to their learning experience. |
| Never Say "No" | While the mentorship process is set, the content and direction are not. Quite often the initiative undertaken by the mentee morphs into other directions and opportunities. This is a natural outcome of progressively fine-tuning anticipated outcomes and expected end results. |
| Positive Psychology | A mentee undertakes the mentorship process because they are unsure or insecure about their endeavors. It is the mentor's responsibility to maintain a positive and encouraging attitude to minimize any of the mentee's self-doubt, and do so without just being a 'yes' person or over-exuberant cheerleader. |
| Managing the Mentor's Load of Mentees | Part of the planning and delivery process is to assure the mentor has allocated sufficient time to respond to the needs of each of the mentees in their charge. |

| Completing the Mentoring Process | At a certain stage, if everything goes as planned, both parties recognize that the process has arrived at a point of self-sufficiency. Little additional coaching is needed. There is a strategy to end the experience properly and track what has been accomplished.<br>• *The Mentee's Report Card Assessing the Mentor*<br>• *Mentoring Adventures and Misadventures* |
|---|---|
| When to Refuse to Mentor Someone | For a limited number of reasons, there may be justification for the mentor to reject a mentee. All the prescreening and assessment/checklists tools provided within the book also safeguard against entering into any flawed coaching relationship. |
| | **CHAPTER 5—Corporate and Academic Mentoring Strategies** |
| Corporate Mentorship Game-planning | Mentorship within the corporate environment is an integral part of teambuilding whereby more experienced managers and executives take some of the "young guns" under their wings. This often includes conveying the corporate vision and strategic operations to those coming up in the ranks. Or the reverse, where the older team learns new strategies and technologies from the newcomers. These are only two examples of corporate mentoring. There are more.<br>*Peer-to-Peer Mentoring*<br>• *Using Mentoring Software*<br>• *Reverse Mentoring*<br>• *Accountability Mentoring*<br>• *Boot Camp Mentoring*<br>• *Mentoring on the Fly*<br>• *Connection-Building Mentoring*<br>• *Mentoring Within the Small Business* |
| Business Mentoring in Academia | The academic world represents a cornerstone in teaching business and entrepreneurship. Training and mentoring are inherent building blocks. Universities offer a myriad of courses and mentoring opportunities or affiliate themselves with well-recognized mentorship associations and service providers. |
| How Mentoring Has Changed | Mentorship has morphed to accommodate changes in the business climate. The rules of engagement and use of platforms such as Zoom and MS Team have created new avenues in which mentorship thrives. However, the very core values of mentorship remain steadfast. |
| | **CHAPTER 6—Mentoring as a Fees-for-Services Business** |

| The Fee-Based Mentor | Delivering mentoring services on a fee basis is part of many professionals' portfolios; business consultants, trainers accountants, and lawyers. This chapter offers "coaching for coaches;" creating revenues and profit centers, subcontracting, the use of virtual trainers, legal issues, and other factors that can help the fee-based mentors grow their practices. |
|---|---|
| | **BONUS – More Mentorship Tools and Lessons** |
| Experience Is a Great Teacher | Includes many mentoring stories and the lessons derived from each experience. |
| A Retrospective: The Author's Own Mentoring World | The author presents a cornucopia of somewhat unique and often "odd" mentoring experiences, and useful, useable lessons learned. |
| Appendix 1 | Mentoring video resources: learn from other experts, from Ted Talks to powerful video mentoring/coaching featuring successful, recognized mentors. |
| Appendix 2 | Mentoring resources and learning through role models, networking associations, conferences, academic programs, online courses, and software. |

# Introduction

*There is no way I could have gotten through that on my own without asking you for help every single step of the way. I now know what my business dream and focus are, because of you. I raise my hands in thanks.*

— "Thank you" note from one of the author's mentees, Cristina A.

## Mentoring

Mentoring is about all sorts of techniques, vision-building, hand-holding, numbers-crunching, and encouragement, but mostly it's about buying into someone else's vision.

If anyone wants to know what business mentoring is all about, reread the above quote and visualize being there when that someone under your mentoring tutelage reaches their entrepreneurial destination. It's an outstanding "wow" moment for you both.

There are hard and soft sides of mentoring, and a balance between the two is crucial. Mentoring is not all about "You need to do it this way, my way," but more so, "Tell me what you are trying to do and where you want this opportunity to take you." It's a sojourn for the mentor as the tour guide and the mentee as the journeyer.

## Who Best Delivers Mentoring?

Business mentoring is best taught by someone with entrepreneurial experience, someone who has also mentored others. Lots of others.

*Powerhouse Business Mentorship* strategies are offered up in this handbook by Jay J. Silverberg who has, for over 35 years, mentored countless entrepreneurs, newbies, business tire kickers, well-established businesspeople, and managers from start-ups to multinationals. Some relationships were great experiences with excellent outcomes, some merely good, and others best described as "colorful."

Mentoring is a tiptoe dance identifying and circumventing roadblocks, assuming a role with responsibilities for each party, developing a close bond, and culminating in a measurable synergy between the mentor and the mentee.

## Mentoring and Being Mentored

Mentoring is a team sport, but each players' interests and intents are different.

1. The **business mentor** guides any prospective (or established) entrepreneur toward meeting their own unique wants, needs, and anticipated business outcomes.
2. The **mentee** needs to be a proactive partner in the mentorship odyssey.

*Powerhouse Business Mentorship* **offers the mentor and the mentee a veritable plentitude of "how to" proprietary resources**; checklists, templates, mentoring contracts, scorecards, and mentorship tracking models, all couched in useable formats.

## Mentorship Defined for All Participants

The Powerhouse Mentorship Handbook is intentionally divided into six chapters, each examining the journey from different perspectives.

### Chapter 1: What Exactly Is Mentorship?

How is mentoring defined from various parties' vantage points, and how it impacts both participants? What are its objectives? What constitutes a successful mentorship journey? Assuring the process is doable, realizable, and is not being inadvertently set up for failure? Overshooting is tantamount to disappointment. These concepts are thoroughly covered in this chapter.

### Chapter 2: The Mentor

Defining the mentors' role. This book is intended for anyone delivering university/diploma-level business or entrepreneurship programs, workshops or simply training would-be businesspeople.

I count myself as a raconteur of entrepreneurial mentoring adventures. Many of the gems of advice and recommendations herein are accompanied by stories about my successful escapades as well as my valiant efforts, some of which, in hindsight, were often joyfully entertaining, but possibly less terribly productive.

Mentoring can sometimes be a calculated leap in the dark.

## Chapter 3: The Mentee

For entrepreneurs seeking out mentorship, this book provides advice on how to find, select, and work with mentors; the kind of features, experience, and compassion to expect; mentoring etiquette, and; how to structure a program that works for you. The mentee's responsibilities and mindset in the mentorship process involve building trust, accepting advice, and assuring the creation of a symbiotic relationship.

## Chapter 4: Gameplanning the Mentorship Journey

In the gameplanning section, the book works to create the optimum conditions for establishing effective mentorship journeys. That includes the "how to" as well as the "how not to." Both are equally important for all stakeholders to understand and remain cognizant of. This chapter includes defining the roles and responsibilities of each party, and how to build an effective working relationship capable of delivering quantifiable results. Defining the rules of engagement is the foundation of gameplanning a workable mentorship process for all parties.

- Which mentorship delivery model best encourages learning and listening?
- What exactly does the mentee expect and how is that matched with the ability of the mentor to meet those expectations (or something in close proximity)?
- Understanding how important mentoring is to the mentee(s) and how it impacts their business decision-making.
- There is a need to assure that the mentee does not perceive the mentor as an "immovable bulldozer." It's a narrow line

between mentoring and bullying, or pushing too soon or too fast for results.

- Learning how both parties "playing nice" is a critical component of mentorship.
- It is sometimes far too tempting for mentors to play God. Mentoring with a deity can shut the mentee down. How to keep the mentor's ego in check, and use that same power to motivate, guide, and inspire the mentee is keynote.
- Mentee honesty and openness encourage the mentor to listen and learn, and to walk in the mentee's shoes for a while. It is quite revealing.
- Getting buy-in from the mentee is crucial. How and when do you do that effectively?
- Maintaining some impartiality. The mentor is the gatekeeper, buying in as an advisor and sounding board without getting too personally involved. Maintaining the "spectator mode" with a certain degree of aloofness.
- Balancing expectations. Creating an understanding that the venture sought by the mentee may be different from the business that results from mentoring, planning, and brainstorming. This is the "moving target switch-over syndrome."
- Guiding, but not destroying, the mentee's dream.
- Sometimes, from either party's perspective, mentoring does not work. When it doesn't, or falters, how do you turn it around or simply walk away?

### Chapter 5: Corporate and Academic Mentoring Strategies

A company's experienced managers may take the new generation under their tutelage, passing along strategic corporate values, and future-forward vision, based on the successes of the past. Any corporation that subscribes to the mentoring process will find this handbook useful for their mentors and mentees. This is also a "how to" handbook with ideas on structuring successful corporate mentoring models.

The academic world is discussed as a host for valuable mentorship opportunities, programs, and activities. Academia is an ideal environment for delivering mentorship programs. This handbook can be a useful resource for academia-based mentors, mentees, trainers, and teachers.

### Chapter 6: Mentoring as a Fees-for-Services Business

This chapter provides advice for the business professional/consultant who may offer mentoring on a fees-for-services basis. This guidance encompasses key aspects of starting, running, and marketing a business mentoring and training consulting company, including the more "mercenary" aspects of contracts, billing, subcontracting, collecting accounts, and avoiding the pitfalls of which there are an abundance. Trust me.

## The Power of the Past

Each topic is also preceded by a quote on the act of mentorship. Why? Because mentorship is a very human and delicate interaction between people and is often expressed in a statement of inspiration, thanks, and reflection.

# CHAPTER 1

# What Exactly Is Mentorship?

*Show me a successful individual and I'll show you someone who had real positive influences in his or her life. I don't **care** what you do for a living—if you do it well, I'm sure there was someone cheering you on or showing the way. A mentor.*

—Denzel Washington

## Mentorship

Keeping one foot on the gas pedal and the other hovering over the brakes, mentorship is a journey of balance. It's the ultimate synergistic experience.

Both parties teach **and** learn the mentoring experience. It's an equal-opportunity, two-way adventure. Neither party positions itself for control, yet both direct, steer, and manipulate the process.

Mentorship is about outcomes; otherwise, it's just a couple of people sharing a coffee and talking shallow-speak. There needs to be a communication link steeped in honest exchange.

The mentor has the responsibility of laying the groundwork; the rules, the "how to," and the very clear definition that they are there to "help" but not "do the work that the mentee needs to do." More on that later. The best mentors lead without leading. Emperor Napoleon Bonaparte inferred that *"firmness can be couched with outward gentleness."*\* So very perfect.

---

\* www.forbes.com/sites/forbescoachescouncil/2021/06/17/balanced-communication-is-it-an-iron-fist-in-a-velvet-glove/?sh=17932cd3c590 .

```
┌─────────────────────────────┐
│      Mentorship Model       │
└─────────────────────────────┘
```

┌──────────────┐
│   Focussed   │
│   and Goal   │
│   Oriented   │
└──────────────┘

┌──────────────┐                    ┌──────────────┐
│ Build Trust, │                    │   Support,   │
│   Rapport,   │                    │  Encourage,  │
│    Opens     │                    │   Guidance   │
└──────────────┘                    └──────────────┘

┌──────────────┐                    ┌──────────────┐
│    Advice,   │                    │  Personal,   │
│   Counsel,   │                    │   Lead by    │
│   Training   │                    │   Example    │
└──────────────┘                    └──────────────┘

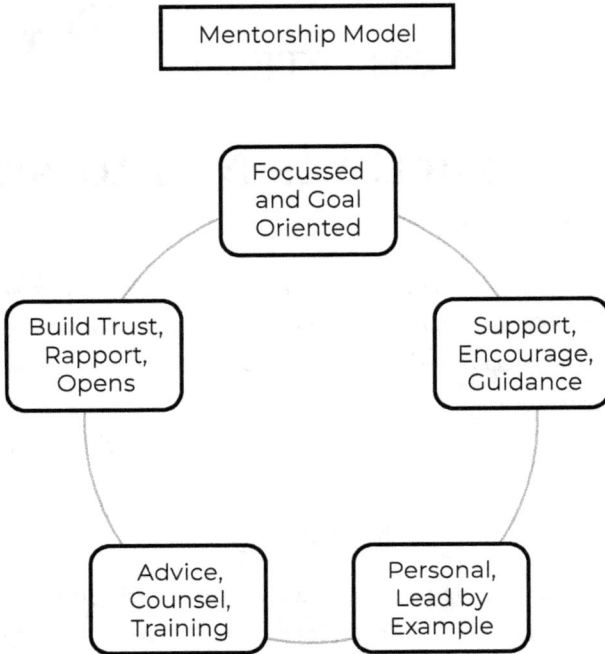

*Source:* This chart was created by the author.

The mentor who pitches their version of what they feel the mentee needs instead of what the participant wants is carrying on "ego/high horse" mentoring, lecturing instead of responding, incorrectly assuming that they, the mentor, know everything while the lowly mentee knows pathetically little. This is arrogant at best and unfulfilling at worst. It's indicative of a relationship that is going in circles, chasing its tail as what is offered up gets rejected, then regurgitated and offered again by the mentor, then more emphatically shunned by the mentee, then ... you can see where this is heading toward self-destruction. Don't let yourself fall into that quagmire.

## Mentorship Provides and Delivers

Mentorship implies building a close relationship between the two parties while maintaining a safe distance for the mentor to maintain their objectivity.

| Mentor Provides | Mentee Receives |
|---|---|
| Business acumen and counsel steeped in experience, leading by example | Training, to whatever degree is required, to fill in any gaps in the mentee's knowledge base |
| A sounding board for entrepreneurs | Goal setting |
| Responding with a clear understanding of the mentee's needs | Motivation |
| Often, a shoulder to lean on, especially in difficult decision-making times | Direction |
| Being a cheerleader | A shared business birthing or growth experience |
| Able to say 'not quite that direction' when it might be difficult but doable to reshape and revamp in the best interest of realizing on the opportunity | Focus and goal setting, keeping projects on track |
| Build on the mentee's strengths while managing their weaknesses and gaps in their business planning | Fulfilling a mentee's vision by being a companion on the entrepreneurial journey |
| Able to challenge the mentee to develop new skills, see alternate opportunities, and keep tight control on the pathway to success | Comfort, in being ever-present for the mentee and providing input both on a scheduled mentoring basis as well as ad hoc, as may be required |
| Learning opportunities provided to the mentor by the mentee | Practical strategies for success |
| | Possible networking opportunities such as connection to funders, investors, distribution channels, and strategic partners |

The mentee, for their part, needs to keep their sensitivities and insecurities under lock and key.

- It's kind of like going into the hospital for a procedure. Very personal. Possibly quite invasive, but the focus is on the moment, getting results without carrying extra baggage.
- The constructive dialog and sharing best exemplify mentoring.
- Resistance to change and deflecting others' viewpoints that differ from yours need to be left at the door.
- It only works if you want it to work.

This is an oversimplification/birds-eye view of the mentoring launch. But nothing is ever that easy. There really is a process to all of this, from inauguration to implementation and reaping the rewards.

## Why Mentorship Succeeds

*Advice is like snow; the softer it falls, the longer it dwells upon, and the deeper it sinks into the mind.*

—Samuel Taylor Coleridge

There are innumerable reasons why a mentorship experience works, but it all starts with an effective matchup between mentor and mentee. The magic of effective communication between parties on the same wavelength and sharing the same purpose can be magical.

Here are other key factors resulting in the success of the mentoring process:

Where the mentor has real-life experience to share, the chances for success are far greater. Books and digital media can only go so far in providing guidance. Hands-on knowledge and know-how represent a maturity of knowledge and wisdom that deliver a kind of mentoring help greater than any other source of counsel.

Conveying experience also implies sharing unwritten stories, strategies, advice, and even warnings that authors may or may not disclose in books. This author's own collection of business books published by Business Expert Press are prime examples of offering advice that goes well beyond the commonplace.[†1]

Mentoring works. Statistics (updated for 2023) demonstrate the value and effectiveness of the process as a pathway for the mentee achieving greater success by participating in structured mentoring.[‡]

- 97 percent of businesspeople who have been mentored say that the experience has been valuable.[§]
- 89 percent of people mentored go on to mentor others. This reflects the success of the process.

---

[†] www.businessexpertpress.com/jay-j-silverberg/.

[‡] https://guider-ai.com/blog/mentoring-statistics-the-research-you-need-to-know/.

[§] https://nationalmentoringday.org/facts-and-statistics/.

- In the Harvard Business Review (2015), 84 percent of participants claimed mentoring helped them avoid costly mistakes, 84 percent acknowledged greater efficiency in their roles, and 69 percent enhanced their decision-making. As well, 70 percent of study participants have stated that sharing their goals with a mentor keeps them accountable and better able to realize their aspirations.[*]
- According to the Small Business Administration, while 30 percent of new businesses fail within twenty-four months, fifty percent of businesses that receive mentoring survive beyond that, and 70 percent thrive beyond five years.[**]

Statistics such as these are indicative that mentees accessing mentorship is a proven and well-documented resource contributing to their success and longevity.

For entrepreneurs seeking "connections" such as funding, investors, and market penetration, mentors can often provide personal contacts. Warm, fuzzy introductions are invaluable. They represent referrals from a trusted source.

Effective mentorship, where there is "give and take" between the parties and a healthy respect for each other's commitment and capabilities, yields a host of additional reasons why mentoring works.

- Greater focus on the issues that truly matter and less so on fluffier subjects that deflect from the ultimate goals sought.
- Provides thinking "outside the box".
- Increases decisiveness based on rational and shared thinking.
- Minimizes or avoids negative moves the mentee may make when left to their own accord.
- Confidence-building wins over almost everything.
- Faster turn-around on decision-making.
- Mentoring provides persistence for the mentee to deal with issues and face what needs to get done.

---

[*]   https://mccarthymentoring.com/why-mentoring-what-the-stats-say/.

[**]   www.sba.gov/.

- Real-time feedback is invaluable.
- The encouragement offered in an effective mentoring scenario is a driving force.
- Mentoring improves the mentees "emotional intelligence" (EI), self-awareness, self-management, social awareness, and relationship management. The end result is a better-rounded entrepreneur who can deal with the challenges and opportunities that business offers.

Mentoring works when both parties want it to work and when they fully immerse themselves.

# Why Mentorship Fails

*Mentors have a way of seeing more of our faults than we would like. It's the only way we grow.*

—George Lucas

There is always the philosophical approach that sometimes, despite the best of intentions, mentoring just does not work. But delving more deeply allows us to identify where that "sometimes" is and, in knowing, helps both the mentor and the mentee to avoid the pitfalls.

- Just as a great match between mentor and mentee works magic, a poor **matchup** is lost before it starts. It is imperative that both parties build that comfort and trust level before embarking on the mentorship journey. Otherwise, it could be an express train with no destination.
- As touched on in a later chapter, there are three levels of **human interaction**: parent to child in a child's formative years; parent to adult as the relationship matures; and child to parent as the connection reverses and the child becomes the alpha grownup. Mentoring demands equality, and if the relationship is anything other than parent-to-adult, then it is doomed.
- **Personalities** come into play. If one party is bull-headed, stubborn, arrogant, or unreceptive, then the process comes to a screeching halt. Nothing gets done.
- **Attitude is critical**. Both parties need to be convinced that the process works or will work. Failing that, every suggestion or action offered will be questioned to death as resistance to advice and counsel grinds down the willpower and interest of both participants or either party. "I believe" is the rallying cry of the successful program.
- **Setting goals is more than a catchphrase**. While it is true that goals can morph, mature, and change as a project starts to find its footing, any significant shifts that create a lack of clarity and purpose will have a detrimental impact on the

mentorship journey. It will also feed conflict and lack of focus between parties. Both participants need to be on the same pathway.

- The **overzealous** or over anxious mentee can steer the process off track. They may ignore warning signs or opportunities, or they may be too eager to reach the goalpost. Likely, they will stumble along the way. Nothing destroys the willpower and drive to succeed more than having to return to the starting line or backtrack a number of steps to redo it all properly.

- **Direction** is key, and creativity needs to be a co-pilot. While creativity is important, improvising is dangerous. "Flying by the seat of your pants" is fine for, say, mountain biking, but is an impediment to mentorship.

- **Collaboration**, getting along, and respect for each other's input is crucial. If any of these are not present, there will be a slim chance of a successful mentoring experience.

- A lack of **understanding of what the process entails** and demands is a certain mentorship killer. The mentee who enters into this blindly is generally surprised that the results are not immediate or quickly reachable. Some pain is part of mentorship and helps participants appreciate the work.

- **Bottlenecks cause issues.** In one instance, my mentee was supposed to develop a pricing structure based on the ingredients in their product. A reasonable request, right? Yet the delivery on their part of this very basic information caused the mentoring progress to grind to a thundering halt. There was nothing to talk about until they did what they committed to doing. Limbo led to a natural death. Mentoring cannot stay in place forever. Projects simply tire out.

- Each project and mentee are different. Offering up a **generic gameplan is rarely well received**. It equates to getting mail addressed to "Dear Occupant."

- Being part of the process is critical. **Buy-in is critical.** The mentee needs to participate, not miss too many scheduled sessions (some are unavoidable), and be well prepared for each, with homework completed. There are numerous benefits associated with participating. There is only one associated directly with non participation. Obscurity.

- **Feedback** is critical, and that is two-way: constructive criticism by the mentor and commentary by the mentee on how the process is going and how well the mentor is fueling the momentum and delivering their services. Lack of either will quickly deteriorate into a "who cares" non alliance.
- A lack of **competence** on behalf of the mentor will reflect on the process, as will the mentor taking on too many mentees and limiting their availability or offering counsel on topics outside their areas of expertise. The outcomes of any of these cannot be good.

Generally, mentorship failures can be avoided by gauging the interests of the other party.

# The Mentoring Scorecard

*The mind is not a vessel that needs filling, but wood that needs igniting.*
— Plutarch

I have had my share of successes and failures, and, aside from any entertainment value when the process simply explodes or immolates, all mentorship experiences are a learning curve for the mentor.

That is how I have always treated it. For the mentor, experience builds a toolbox of resources and know-how.

Here are **three real-life examples chosen to illustrate "good, bad, and ugly" session-by-session mentoring undertakings**. They are unfiltered, except for the personal information about the mentees.

As well, the conclusion of each example will include a **Mentoring Scorecard**, which is a tool I have developed to catalog my experiences. Feel free to use this in your own mentoring practice. Here is what an example looks like:

| (Blank Template) Mentoring Scorecard | | |
|---|---|---|
| **Mentoring Outcomes** | **Notes** | **Scores 1 (−) to 5 (+)** |
| | (Note: in this template illustration, the descriptive notes below are to help the mentor grade their mentoring experience) | |
| Opening dialog | Able to share their vision and purpose of mentoring, understands how the program works | |
| Project description clear | Mentee has a well-defined initiative and is capable of conveying their thoughts | |
| Goal setting and targets | Clear and prioritized. Realistic. Likely achievable | |
| Timetables established | Set regular Zoom meeting schedule with sufficient intervals for mentee to carry out their "homework" | |
| Homework assignments | Well received and mostly completed in a timely manner | |
| Trust | Mutual trust and respect exhibited. The relationship clicks | |

*(Continued)*

| (Blank Template) Mentoring Scorecard | | |
|---|---|---|
| **Mentoring Outcomes** | **Notes** | **Scores 1 (−) to 5 (+)** |
| Effective communications | Transparent and mutual two-way connection | |
| Milestones clarified | Action plan agreed upon with specific timelines and milestones set | |
| Milestones met | Action items mostly met and new targets set for those not achieved | |
| Definable progress | Quantifiable and measurable progress at each session | |
| Mutual feedback | Open forum for two-way feedback | |
| Mentoring completed | Goals mostly met. Mentoring successful | |
| Follow up done | Follow up schedule set | |

### The Good Mentoring Experience

Drake, young tech, age 29, well educated, marginal entrepreneurial experience, software game app project.

1. SESSION 1—Good introductions all around; seems very focused and goal-oriented.
2. SESSION 2—Drake presented their early draft Business Plan for discussion. Short on market and target market/demographics research. Suggested they carry this out and offered up some research techniques and avenues.
3. SESSIONS 3,4—Discussed their findings, and started narrowing down the scope of their opportunity and what it takes to get there. Identified potential roadblocks and how to navigate them.
4. SESSION 5—Reviewed their startup needs both in terms of costs and human resources (capable sub-contractors). Suggested they carry out a SWOT analysis (strengths, weaknesses, opportunities, and threats) with a focus on risks.
5. SESSION 6—Reviewed and questioned their SWOT analysis, which they defended well. Delved into their personal and family lives only to inquire about their support mechanisms.

6. SESSION 7—Drake was asked to present at least three "what if" scenarios ranging between a very successful launch and a "do-over." They seemed to have a good grasp on where this initiative may be heading.

7. SESSION 8—I played the role of the funder and blitzed Drake with tough questions, most of which they fielded. Spent time fine-tuning their presentation style and content in line with what funders generally need to hear. Helped design the format for a PowerPoint Deck.

8. SESSION 9—Introduced Drake to three funding managers within my network.

9. SESSION 10—Drake completed the mentoring series and was off on their own.

10. SESSION 11—Followed up with Drake in months 4 and 8 post-launch. Drake seemed to be doing just fine. Questions were dealt with. Feedback on my style was offered up by Drake, and that proved useful.

| Drake Mentoring Scorecard | |
|---|---|
| Mentoring Outcomes | Scores 1 (−) to 5 (+) |
| | |
| Opening dialog | 5 |
| Project description clear | 5 |
| Goal setting and targets | 4 |
| Timetables established | 5 |
| Homework assignments | 4 |
| Trust | 5 |
| Effective communications | 5 |
| Milestones clarified | 4 |
| Milestones met | 4 |
| Definable progress | 5 |
| Mutual feedback | 4 |
| Mentoring completed | 5 |
| Follow-up done | 5 |

## The Bad Mentoring Experience

Dusty and Cheyenne, partners, both in their early thirties, were involved in starting an entertainment company, party rentals, disc jockeys, and event staging

1. SESSION 1—Sensed immediately that there was some friction between them and they were not being transparent with me. Their ideas were not in parallel.
2. SESSION 2—Spent most of the session defending myself, my experience, and my abilities. It was an uncomfortable shift of focus. They transferred some of their hostilities to me.
3. SESSION 3—Designed the outline of important market research they needed to do before investing all their funds, which, in itself, was identified by me as a risk.
4. SESSION 4—Reviewed their research, which was sketchy and incomplete at best. Dusty did not have the time to do anything.
5. SESSION 5—Discussed and presented the outline for a Business Plan and budget which, they were told, they would need to complete before a funder would look at them. Not well received.
6. SESSION 6—Nothing done by either. Watched as the two of them got into a squabble about the vision of the company they were trying to launch. Suggested we put things on hold until they reached some consensus, without which I could not help.
7. SESSION 7—The mentorship program was restarted several months down the road. Both parties seemed more amenable to the process and shared a common goal. Together, we developed a gameplan to follow through and rekindle the mentoring. I adapted my style to tiptoe between their areas of disagreement, which still clouded the process. However, there was progress.
8. SESSIONS 8, 9, and 10—Progress in baby steps seemed to work, particularly without any issues that caused friction. All personal dealings regarding their non business relationship were avoided.
9. SESSION 11—Arrived at a point where the excitement of the venture exceeded the personal quibbling. The business launched and did well. This started off badly, was salvaged and became a success story.

| Dusty and Cheyenne Mentoring Scorecard | |
|---|---|
| Mentoring Outcomes | Scores 1 (−) to 5 (+) |
| | |
| Opening dialog | 3 |
| Project description clear | 3 |
| Goal setting and targets | 2 |
| Timetables established | 3 |
| Homework assignments | 2 |
| Trust | 3 |
| Effective communications | 3 |
| Milestones clarified | 2 |
| Milestones met | 4 |
| Definable progress | 4 |
| Mutual feedback | 4 |
| Mentoring completed | 5 |

### The Ugly Mentoring Experience

Candice, thirty-something, outdoorsy/back-to-nature type, interested in an all-natural cosmetics line. Some marginal experience in the healthcare products sector.

1. SESSION 1—Hesitant to share, concerned about trade secrets despite a signed NDA given to her.
2. SESSION 2—Discussed her limited entrepreneurial experience. Her drive seemed to be fueled primarily out of curiosity for business.
3. SESSION 3—Worked to build confidence and trust by explaining my background and experience in the field. Defiance. "Why should I trust you, or anyone else?" Paranoia. Meeting ended early. No real avenue to pursue.
4. SESSION 4—No show. I attempted to rekindle the process but was again rebuffed. Closed the file.

| Dusty Mentoring Scorecard | |
|---|---|
| **Mentoring Outcomes** | **Scores 1 (−) to 5 (+)** |
| | |
| Opening dialog | 1 |
| Project description clear | 2 |
| Goal setting and targets | 1 |
| Timetables established | - |
| Homework assignments | - |
| Trust | Combative |
| Effective communications | None |
| Milestones clarfied | - |
| Milestones met | - |
| Definable progress | - |
| Mutual feedback | - |
| Mentoring completed | Abandoned |

As you can see, mentoring experiences range from the wonderful to the pitiful.

The effective mentor will ascertain the viability of any particular prospective mentee and determine strategies for moving forward or identifying roadblocks, some of which might be impassible. **Don't waste your time on any relationships that you just know are sublimely difficult or doomed from the get-go.**

## The Origin of the "Mentor"

There is an oft-quoted interesting reference throughout studies and resource materials as relating to the source of "mentor," and how the process of knowledge-sharing between mentor and mentee developed.[††]

*In Homer's great poem "The Odyssey" (800 BCE.), Odysseus had a tough time finding his way home to his palace in Ithaca after the Trojan War, what with all those monsters, dangerous whirlpools, Sirens and Lotus Eaters threatening to derail his journey. But Odysseus at least had the comfort of knowing that he had left a wise and trusted fellow named Mentor to be the guardian and teacher of his son.*

The tradition has carried on through the ages. The concept of "passing on" knowledge continues and flourishes.

---

[††] "Knowledge at Wharton Podcast: Workplace Loyalties Change, but the Value of Mentoring Doesn't," Wharton School, University of Pennsylvania. https://knowledge.wharton.upenn.edu/podcast/knowledge-at-wharton-podcast/workplace-loyalties-change-but-the-value-of-mentoring-doesnt/.

## Mentoring Adventures and Misadventures

I once hired a marketing consultant to help one of my clients expand her cosmetic skincare line to other licensed vendors. That was the mandate, nothing more.

Her products were selling well, and she had built up an impressive cult-like following, mainly because the skin cream did exactly as advertised, and she was a born promoter. Plus, she was super comfortable that her packaging, brand, and pitch were all working marvelously.

Enter the marketing guru. Instead of following my directives and those of my client, he insisted that the company needed a full marketing makeover, brand, and image, even though it was already successful. He remained oblivious to the specific needs and stayed stubbornly focused on what he erroneously perceived as the clients' needs.

The clashes were endless and progressively deteriorated into mudslinging bouts. As you can imagine, it did not end well. The consultant was fired, and I undertook to reinstate my own good will, which had suffered in the melee.

I should have recognized earlier on that the mentee was not being served, but, instead, was being bullied into submission. When a mentee deflects advice and counsel, even if you think it's correct, you need to stop and listen. Listening is actually one of the cornerstones of mentoring.

Consider each mentorship journey as an opportunity for you, yourself, to become a better businessperson.

# CHAPTER 2

# The Mentor

*If you cannot see where you are going, ask someone who has been there.*

—J. Loren Norris

## Are You Mentoring Material?

Mentoring isn't for everybody. In fact, it takes professional and personal strengths (and sacrifice) to deliver the role effectively. Throw mentee insecurities into the equation and you will certainly be challenged.

The tasks and the responsibilities are onerous, but the benefits to you will be ginormous. In business, there is little that equates to being part of a success, even someone else's, one that you supported and co-nurtured.

However, this begs the question "**Are you mentoring material**?" Take the test (below). Respond "Yes/Of Course" if this describes you. Respond "Needs Work" if it doesn't quite fit, but you can think of ways you can shore up your mentorship shortfall(s).

At the same time, you can use this chapter as a preliminary yardstick to decide if you want to embark on the mentoring pathway where payment is generally measured in "thank you."

| Mentoring "Stick-to-it-Ness" Skills | Of Course, This Describes Me | One of My Shortfalls I Can Work On |
|---|---|---|
| PATIENCE AND PERSISTENCE | | |
| Good listener | | |
| Nonjudgmental | | |
| "Staying power" if progress is 3 steps forward and 2 steps backward | | |

(Continued)

| Mentoring "Stick-to-it-Ness" Skills | Of Course, This Describes Me | One of My Shortfalls I Can Work On |
|---|---|---|
| Able to shape-shift to build a comfort level with the mentee | | |
| Thick-skinned, especially if mentee pays little heed to your advice, misses task deadlines or glosses over your sage counsel | | |
| Persistence | | |
| Able to build trust quickly | | |
| Availability, often at inconvenient times | | |
| Positive attitude that communicates well to others | | |
| Cheerleader capabilities | | |
| Inspirational, moves mentee to action | | |
| Responsive | | |
| Emotional and proactive | | |
| See mentees as equals-in-training | | |
| Painfully honest without inflicting undue pain | | |
| Zeroes in on mentee goals and needs | | |
| Able to discard the "fluff" and focus on key issues | | |
| Strong core skills | | |
| Enjoy the training process | | |
| Previous mentoring experience is a plus | | |
| Great storyteller to instill "how to" lessons | | |
| Respond to feedback from mentee, including regarding your style and communication skills | | |
| Can pivot as situations demand it | | |
| Open to learning. Mentoring is often a two-way process. | | |
| Exude confidence. Your ego does not always need to be stroked. | | |

(Continued)

| Mentoring "Stick-to-it-Ness" Skills | Of Course, This Describes Me | One of My Shortfalls I Can Work On |
|---|---|---|
| Malleable attitude responsive to project changes and shifts which often happen along the mentoring journey | | |
| Organized, especially if juggling several mentees | | |
| Able to acknowledge when things simply don't work out | | |

Done? Great! Now show your responses to someone who knows you well and get their take on whether you have been perfectly honest with yourself, or some "tweaking" is needed.

Find ways to improve any feature under the "shortfalls" column.

# Defining Your Core Mentoring Skills

*A mentor is someone who can give you guidance, advice, and support when you need it.*

—Richard Branson

There are a number of mentoring skills that go well beyond the catch-phrases like "helping others" and "being a sounding board." These are often referred to as "core" skills.

These "core" skills will separate you from the gurus and sages who may simply float through the mentoring process while leaving little of value behind. One of the definable results of effective mentoring is that you will have added value to someone's business venture and their ability to personally undertake and succeed in their enterprise.

Adopting or simply fine-tuning your in-depth core skills will dramatically enhance your modus operandi in how you deliver quantifiable results for your charges.

## The Two-Way Relationship

While it may appear that mentoring is a one-way deal, it is not. It demands a lot from both parties who recognize what each brings to the relationship.

Mentoring is sharing someone else's dreams and aspirations. It is critical that as much as the mentee opens up to you, that you, in turn, demonstrate the kind of interest and commitment that is demanded of you.

## Being on the Same Wavelength

Every mentor-mentee relationship is unique because people come with "baggage" that impacts their ability to teach and learn. Both parties being on the same wavelength is critical, as is their being attuned to each other's expected outcome from the process.

Commonality is critical.

Connecting via effective communication not only includes you providing the counsel and advice that the mentee needs but extends to exhibiting your synergy via body language, eye contact, follow-up, and sincere interest in what they are doing. Pay attention.

### Parent-to-Adult Connection

As children, we build parent-child relationships. Our parents care for us, feed us, teach us, and keep us safe. We are the dependents in the relationship.

As seniors, we reverse the relationship and we become the children while our grown adult kids take on the caretaking role.

In between, there is a period of parent-adult interaction, where we are equals in how we treat each other, build trust and understanding, which evolves into a mutually beneficial bond. The parent-adult phase of interaction is the one that works between a mentor and a mentee.

Treat your mentee with mutual respect, adopting personal boundaries and creating a working environment that delivers quantifiable benefits.

Remember that everyone receives input differently, so be sensitive to how advice is offered and received. Lecturing a mentee who is fragile is a sure way to terminate the process.

Far too often mentors will adopt an ivory tower, haughty know-it-all approach with mentees that reverts the relationship to parent-child. Don't go there. It defeats the process. As my grandson was fond of saying "I can't hear you. I shut my ears."

### Be an Attentive Listener

*"When you talk, you are only repeating what you already know. But if you listen, you may learn something new."*

—Dalai Lama

Listening is something we take for granted. Listening is easy. Hearing what is being said is more difficult still.

Establishing open communication means hearing what each other is saying; the mentee opening up about their needs, and the mentor responding directly and succinctly without evading the topic. There is no dancing and skating around in hearing one another.

- Cellphones off
- Background noise diminished
- Distractions minimized
- Reflect comments back to mentee to demonstrate you are paying attention
- Nonverbal language to show you are present in the conversation
- Inquire about progress regarding past suggestions and action items agreed to

### Understanding Expectations

Make absolutely certain that the deliverables and results you are targeting are actually what the mentee wants to achieve. Set expectations together, and revisit those goalposts on a regular basis throughout the mentoring process.

Understand what you each want out of the relationship, and agree on the roadmap to get there.

### Devoting Your Time

Every process has a beginning date and needs a completion date. Mentoring cannot go on forever as it develops a dependency on the part of the mentee. Contracts have predetermined end dates. Mentoring should be treated likewise.

Set those yardsticks early on in the process. If the outcomes are not achieved within the timeframe you prescribe, you can renegotiate, but do so with another end date set.

### Building Mutual Trust

Trust implies building a safe environment over time for working through the process. It is the mentor's responsibility to build that key trust. Here's how to do that.

- Empathy. Put yourself in the mentee's place to understand what their expectations, needs, and fears might be.

- Maintain strict confidentiality, and make sure the mentee knows that. Perhaps, a Non disclosure Agreement ("NDA") may comfort the mentee, but it should not really be necessary.
- Time spent together builds trust.
- Be a truth-teller. Lies are usually temporary structures that crumble at the worst time.
- Don't be afraid to admit mistakes. Humility looks good on the mentor.
- When you are at crossroads, you can agree to disagree and move on, returning to the contentious issues later.

### Knowing When to Give Advice

In Hollywood, they often say "timing is everything." In mentoring, the same doctrine applies.

The mentor needs to know when is the appropriate time to offer input/advice or challenge the mentee ONLY when they are ready.

The effective mentor recognizes when input will be well received. It's a matter of knowing your mentee and recognizing when they are most receptive.

Don't rush it.

If your timing skills are honed, any counsel will generally be well received and considered, or at the very least, acknowledged by the mentee.

If your timing is too aggressive, the mentee will feel they are being lectured to and see themselves as the silent, irrelevant partner in the mentorship process.

This goes hand-in-hand with not making assumptions about your mentee, and that includes always thinking you know when you feel the timing is right to interject your thoughts into the conversation. The wrong timing can shut everything down quickly and fatally.

### Being a Resource for the Mentee

Entrepreneurship is about learning, particularly for early-stage businesses. If you gauge that the mentee has certain gaps in their business acumen, it is your responsibility to help them build capacity.

- Resources to refer to, including books, training videos, and/or connecting them to people who can respond to their specific gaps and needs
- Discuss your own experiences or, in general terms, events that helped shape other mentees you have served

### Always Showing Encouragement

Encouragement translates to recognition and appreciation for the grinding work the mentee is doing. This praise does not have to be bubbly and glowing. It means remaining positive and reinforcing the mentee's efforts.

Understand that, quite often, a mentee's ego can be fragile, especially if they are sensitive to the risks of their undertaking and their commitment in time and the costs it takes to strive toward achieving their goals. Psychologically, this plays with the confidence level of the proponent. Encouragement defrays some of the insecurities.

- Even when disagreeing, include the positive, such as "I don't buy into your target market, but I think you are heading in the right direction."
- All correspondence should include an encouraging note.
- Emphasize your interest in working with them.
- Show approval of any positive or professional character traits they have. Favorable comments are always well received.
- Recognize progress and accomplishments. Constantly celebrate achievements along the journey.
- Make sure they don't feel alone in the process.
- Mentees often seek the approval from the mentor. Always be ready to provide it. Share your personal experiences so that they realize their mentor is an ally who has undergone similar challenges and has mitigated them successfully.
- Never make the mentoring experience "you against them."

### Focus, Focus, Focus

The ability to maintain a keen focus "on the prize" is a critical core skill. Vigilance and staying on track are demanded of the mentor.

Often the mentee will be "seduced" by unrealistic goals, major deviations from their original ideas, or get caught up in the glare of new sub opportunities loosely related to their existing project. This is often accompanied by rising project costs, the need to find more funds, a broadened target market beyond the immediately achievable, or the need to bring other stakeholders to the table, which only complicates an opportunity when others' agendas come into play.

The net result is a scenario that is far tougher to implement (if ever).

Focus is the key. The mentor must be the **"reality gatekeeper,"** keeping the mentee attuned to the agreed-upon milestones and goals, and recognizing when the pathway veers off course.

That having been said, things do change, circumstances present themselves that demand change, and subsequently, projects do morph. That often occurs in the normal planning and opportunity implementation stages.

The mentor needs to remain cognizant of these deviations, but not to any degree that represents a disadvantage or risk for the project and the mentee.

Realistic and achievable milestones are key, and maintaining that focus and stability need to be part of the mentor's core skillsets.

### Understanding Your Own Limitations

Be aware of what you can and cannot deliver. Far too often mentors may take on roles where they are less qualified, such as a website programmer doing graphic web content design, or a financial planner undertaking a marketing mentorship role.

Be honest with yourself. Know your limits and abilities, and what value you can bring to a mentoring relationship. Don't undertake assignments that overstep your expertise, and your ability to deliver results.

### The Mentor as the Instructor

The mentor has a natural role, and that is the trainer/instructor who helps build the capacity of the mentee. It is vital the mentor recognizes this responsibility and develops the core skills to enhance the capabilities of their charge.

- Develop the communication skills of a trainer/teacher.
- Provide access to resources, web links, and including others capable of delivering specialized training.
- Wherever feasible, teach by example. Share past experiences, including from other mentorship assignments (while maintaining confidentiality).
- Provide positive reinforcement as the mentee absorbs new knowledge and know-how.

### Two-Way Feedback

While the mentor's primary role is to help the mentee, quite often the mentee will reverse the role by providing feedback to the mentor, even corrective comments regarding the mentor's style, behavior, ability to listen, and delivery.

Learn to be open to "constructive criticism" from the mentee. Let them know this feedback is welcome. This will further reinforce the parent-adult relationship so important in the mentorship.

Assure that any feedback you give or get is specific and includes examples to further explain and explore the issues. Anything that is too generic such as "I don't like the process" will demand some further exploration to mine down to the problems that need to be addressed.

Deal with any feedback quickly so that the mentoring process is not interrupted.

### Parenting and Risk-Adversity

Traditionally, a mentor's role is to protect its offspring, keeping them out of harm's way.

In the same light, the mentor's core skills need to include safeguarding the mentee from any imminent, perceived, or existing dangers.

Hand-in-hand with looking out for the best interests of the mentee is teaching them how and when to avoid unnecessary risks, and, more importantly, learning to recognize mistakes that may be looming on the horizon.

The mentee may well be overthinking the issue which may not be as problematic as they assume. Helping the mentee recognize this is part of the mentor's skillsets, and delivered in a positive "let's deal with it" framework so as to diffuse almost any situation.

Where requested, the mentor can intervene in issues on behalf of the mentee, but caution must be exercised so that the mentor does not possibly become a liable player in the event.

This can be particularly perilous if those issues are of a personal nature (family, marriage, health). Try to limit your involvement and stay armslength in these scenarios.

### The Mentor as the Networker/Connector

Mentors need to have strong networking skills along with an extensive contacts base that can be made available to their mentee charges, including, but not limited to, prospective clients, distributors, funders, investors, tax and financial planning lawyers, accountants, marketing consultants, and human resource experts.

Why? The assumption is that the mentees, particularly new entrepreneurs, early-stage businesses, or companies undergoing change, may lack the wherewithal to liaise with these people without a personal introduction by an established businessperson, and that is you.

The mentor needs to be a willing door opener.

### Roots Mentoring

This is a mentoring strategy designed specifically to determine and break down what may be limiting the mentee's ability to open up and participate in the process.

It may sound like a therapy session, but it is geared toward understanding and dealing with the mentee's inability to share.

Once completed, the more traditional mentoring model can be instituted.

## Using Humor in Mentoring

Humor is an effective ice-breaker. It encourages people to be more open in their communications and has a tendency to provoke greater interaction between the parties.

This is likely my favorite mentoring model. It is one that I employ in most of my communications, including mentoring, as well as group presentations and speaking engagements.

This does not imply telling "did you hear the one about" jokes to impress or entertain, or purposely injecting humor into a conversation. Instead, using humor related directly to what is being discussed at a mentoring session is spontaneous, and subtle and enhances the sense of connection between mentor and mentee. It fosters belonging to the process. It is a sharing moment.

Using humor includes the mentor sharing experiences, both good and bad, that are relevant to the mentee's own journey. It exemplifies the mentor's understanding of the challenges at hand and shows mentors to be "human". It creates a more open and relaxed dialog.

Particularly in encounters that feel stifled or are terse, where the mentee may be feeling insecure or even threatened as the mentor delves with pointed questions, humor lifts the mood and often breaks through the block by creating a stronger emotional connection.

It has been proven that humor inspires and energizes learning, and learning is the core of mentorship.

*Humor activates the brain's dopamine reward system, stimulating goal-oriented motivation and long-term memory ... and can improve retention.**

---

* Teaching Strategies: "Laughter and Learning: Humor Boosts Retention," George Lucas Educational Foundation. www.edutopia.org/blog/laughter-learning-humor-boosts-retention-sarah-henderson.

## Looking After the Mentee's Best Interests

*Mentoring is a brain to pick, an ear to listen, and a push in the right direction.*

—John Crosby

There is one more responsibility that is crucial; looking after their charge's best interests, and keeping them out of trouble.

Quite often, the mentee is blinded by the brilliance of their own entrepreneurial moment. Dancing Christmas sugar plum faeries pirouetting through the mentee's brain, casting piles of money in all directions. It's an inspiring and enlightening image.

However, often the mentee skirts disaster without knowing it. Game-changing challenges or obstructions are downplayed, ignored, or remain concealed behind those pesky faeries, until things strike the proverbial fan. Then it's too late.

During the course of the mentorship journey, there are many secrets revealed. Some critical ones are just glossed over. This kind of complacency can be a deal killer. The toughest part is catching these thorny burrs and, quite often, arm-wrestling the mentee to recognize the red flags and just to deal with them.

## Code of Conduct for Mentors

*I think the greatest thing we give each other is encouragement ... knowing that I'm talking to someone in this mentoring relationship who's interested in the big idea here is very, very important to me. I think if it were just about helping me get to the next step, it would be a heck of a lot less interesting.*

—Anne Sweeney

There is a certain somewhat charming etiquette connected with mentoring, and it applies to all players. What is expected of them? How does their behavior impact the results? When and how to go to that "extra mile?" What is frowned upon? What definitely not to do?

When dealing with mentors and mentees, both strangers entering into the arena, it is imperative to establish guidelines of behavior (and avoidable misbehavior), all of which can and will likely deflate the hoped-for outcomes.

- Value the mentee.
- Look on this experience as a walk side-by-side with a mentee during their business journey.
- Set goals that are the mentees, and not the mentors.
- Respect the mentee and admire their efforts and drive.
- Understand why the mentee has undertaken the journey, what their impetus is; family, financial betterment, escape from the corporate world, need to break out, improving themselves, a learning experience, or anything else. Understanding and appreciating the mentee's motive will make the mentor a better adviser.
- Listen before responding. A quick response reflects the mentor's take, without hearing the mentee out.
- Help mentees make the right decisions and choose their own pathways. Guide them without making decisions for them.
- Encourage self-reliance.

- Teach without lecturing.
- Stay interested and interesting.
- During the mentorship journey, the mentee will develop new skills and abilities. Focus on these as much as the initiative at hand.
- Don't be afraid to ask how you are doing as a mentor, and respond by changing your style if need be.
- Celebrate wins, both the mentees and yours.
- Constructive criticism is a tightrope balancing act. Tread carefully.
- Teach by example. Stories of your experiences and even role playing are effective and can break up any monotony in the process.
- Stick to your areas of expertise. Don't be a know-it-all.
- Focus on the big picture. The little stuff will fall into place.
- Help the mentee question (and hopefully validate) the core assumptions they made for their initiative.
- Be constantly aware of the mentee's style and coach them accordingly to keep their interest. Talk at the same level as the mentee.
- Respect your mentee's time as much as your own.
- Try to ask permission to provide feedback before jumping in headfirst and headstrong.
- Don't expect the mentee to follow all your suggestions. They are ONLY suggestions.
- Conflicts? Develop resolution strategies that keep everything on track.
- Even after the mentoring exercise is completed, keep your door open for future contact.
- Look at this as a two-way learning experience. The mentor learns almost as much as they dish out.
- Think of "realistic optimism" when reflecting on the mentee's aspirations, goals, and plans.

## The Rewards of Mentorship for the Mentor

*If I have seen further it is by standing on the shoulders of giants.*

—Isaac Newton

Mentoring has a profound effect on the mentor, and the "rewards" are bountiful, even multifarious (i.e., assorted, diverse, myriad, various).

It is generally assumed that the main beneficiary of the mentorship is the mentee who benefits from coaching and counsel delivered by an experienced mentor. However, mentoring is a two-way street insofar as perks that accrue to the mentor throughout the journey.

These represent an assemblage of mentor rewards.

Every mentorship contract gives the mentor the opportunity to learn about new industries, varied business sectors, and a range of new areas of opportunity.

Throughout my career, I have become a 'superficial' expert on biotech, resource extraction, retail and franchising, medical resources, advanced software and applications development, healthcare products and services, and entertainment and media, to mention but a few. I could carry on a conversation about any of these, albeit for only a few moments each, such is the superficial nature of dabbling into new territories during the mentoring process. However, I have successfully broadened my scope of knowledge and interest, and that is a definite reward.

Business thrives on networking, and self-employed entrepreneurship even more so. As the mentor opens doors for the mentees, they are expanding their own network. It is an invaluable reward, and a useful asset the mentor accesses for their own business interests. You can never have enough contacts.

Most mentors are highly organized people. However, managing a number of mentees fine-tunes the multitasking capabilities of the mentor. It is elegant stickhandling.

Another benefit/reward to multitasking is developing leadership skills. The mentor becomes a better planner, time allocation specialist, and responsibility delegator, particularly if they bring other sub mentors into the equation to help out.

Two major skills of business are (1) communication and (2) listening before you speak. The mentor cannot help but fine-tune these critical skills. Both are almost art forms that the mentor has an opportunity to practice and apply in their dealings with the mentee. Included is the learned habit of reflecting and weighing their words before responding. Yet another key skill in the mentor's toolbox.

Identifying and suggesting changes and improvements for the mentee provides the mentor with the opportunity of "self-reflection" and identifying areas where they themselves can improve. Any occasions where your response to a situation could have been better? Skills that could use some improvements? Undoubtedly so.

**Mentoring changes peoples' lives. The impact of that is transformational for the mentor. Over the thousands of entrepreneurs I have mentored, I am still overwhelmed when I receive a heartfelt letter of appreciation from a mentee. It still takes my breath away knowing I have improved others' lives. The concept of "giving-back" is addictive.**

Every time the mentor succeeds on behalf of a mentee, there is a definite boost to their own confidence. Endorphins are a wonderful drug.

Of course, there is the reward of recognition as the mentor chalks up successes and their reputation escalates. It is a humbling experience worth pursuing.

The successful mentor develops a greater appreciation for their own value, and what they have to offer. The added-value the mentor provides to their charges nurtures a greater respect for self.

Mentorship is steeped in authenticity and relationship-building. If the mentor can draw from these experiences, that is a distinct reward as well.

Finally, there is the sense of community and membership in an exclusive club of mentors who share the desire to support new generations of entrepreneurs. The rewards of belonging cannot be overstated.

# What Mentors Should NOT Do

- Never assume the role of the ONLY problem solver. This is a shared-responsibility relationship.
- Keep the boundaries rigid. Help the mentee work things out.
- Don't do any of the work that the mentee should be doing or expects you to do. If such expectations are out of line, fix the misunderstanding immediately.
- Guide but don't force mentees into any one direction.
- Overpowering the mentee with your clout and credentials is a no-no. Feed your ego elsewhere.
- Maintain some distance. As a mentor, you have impact. As a friend, the relationship changes dramatically.
- Never condemn or talk down to mentees.
- Limit your mentee load. Having too many charges will decrease your effectiveness with all of them.
- Mentees are not "free labor." Don't give them assignments that you would be doing in your own work, or might be subcontracting out. And don't make personal requests either.
- Micromanaging the mentee just reduces their ability to act on their own. Avoid it.
- The mentee knows their needs or has an inkling of what they need. Try to avoid making assumptions on their behalf. Don't treat mentees like wards.
- The mentees time availability should always be as important as the mentor's own schedule.
- Don't expect, or try to shape the mentee into a clone of yourself. Leave that to cheesy sci-fi movies.
- Try never to end a mentorship on a sour note. Life is too short to rack up disquiet.

# Mentoring Adventures and Misadventures

My client, ABC Company, was involved in providing custom software designs and systems to the federal government. Over the years they had won the high levels of security clearance required for contractors.

A proposal issued by the federal government was almost perfect for ABC Company to bid on. There was just one piece of Intellectual Property ("IP") missing. Coincidentally, they were approached by DEF Company who possessed the IP but did not have the security necessary to bid. One of the benefits of DEF's association with ABC was that they would be granted security clearance as part of the bidding team.

A joint venture was proposed by DEF.

DEF then proposed to add two more companies to the team, both of which DEF held majority shares. Neither of these had security clearance and neither added any discernable value to the proposal. Red flags started cropping up, but ABC Company soldiered on, likely blinded by the profit potential that the contract offered.

DEF Company produced a Memorandum of Understanding that had a liability clause that read "All parties would be responsible, jointly and severally, for any liability issues encountered, client clawbacks, and damages incurred during the delivery of the contract." So, if DEF or their cohorts caused the team to fall short on the deliverables, my client would jointly be on the hook. The red flags kept piling on, but my client still wanted to be in the game.

The final red flag was that one of DEF's associated company's Director was named Andrei Vasilev, an ex-Russian research scientist. In today's troubling times, it was impossible to imagine Andrei getting security clearance, and failure to secure that would cause the entire contract to tumble down, with my client's reputation getting soiled in the process.

I raised the alarms, acting in the best interests of my mentee client.

My client finally tired of my raising this bouquet of red flags, and walked away from the proposed joint venture, but not the bid itself. Another better-qualified strategic partner was identified, the joint bid went it, and my client won the bid without the impediments and dangers caused by the mob of red flags.

Mentoring means more than teaching and sharing knowledge. It also means being a watchdog, diligently watching out for the best interests of the mentee, and speaking up when the voice in your head starts screaming "Danger, Will Robinson, Danger!"

# CHAPTER 3

# The Mentee

*If you want to go fast, go alone. If you want to go far, go together.*
—African Proverb

## Defining the Types of Mentees

You will undoubtedly be dealing with many "types" of mentees, from tire-kickers to dedicated secondary or tertiary growth businesses. The scenarios below represent a cross-section of the mentees you will be dealing with.

**Ready, set, and (almost) go:** By far, the best category of mentees with which to work are the prepared or semi-prepared would-be entrepreneurs. They will have done their research and homework. They have likely qualified their intended business model. They are super-receptive, and your chances of mentoring them to a successful conclusion are highly achievable.

**Stratosphere dreamers:** I have always enjoyed and admired those who see no visible limits or ceiling to their business potential. They are the hardcore dreamers and are the most enthusiastic. If, in the course of mentoring, they can be grounded to reality, they can shine in their enterprise, but need a great deal of attention tethering their ships to Mother Earth.

**The resurrected:** "I have tried this before, but now I have a better idea on how to do it." Great. Do it together, but let's do it right this time around.

**Established, eager, but stuck:** Entrepreneurs who are already in business, but stuck in their plans to expand, retract, divest, diversify, acquire competitors, seek funders/investors/partners, or take any impactful action. Often, they cannot or will not see beyond the blinders that are restricting their moving forward vision. This becomes an exercise in helping to qualify their Business Model * and possibly their new Value Proposition,† assuming they are reaching out to a new marketplace.

**Inspired:** Generally, someone who woke up in the night, or during the course of a daydream, or while watching a Tick Tock, Facebook, YouTube, or LinkedIn video, and was struck by the novelty of an idea which, based on its source, was likely as un-novel as it gets. Really good business ideas rarely get splashed on social media for others to copycat. That does not negate the merit of the opportunity, but usually means the mentee needs to reflect on the idea that has been done by others and is being flogged for all to admire. Over-hyped franchise opportunities are a good example.

**Tire kickers:** There are always those who proclaim, "I am just thinking about it." Don't be fooled. In many instances, these prospective mentees have given their venture ideas a great deal of thought, but are simply circling the bungee jump launching pad, waiting for impetus. You are that impetus.

**The envious ones:** "If they can do it, so can I." Naivety is a fatal condition. Avoid these. Remember, you need to keep your track record of success "healthy," so taking on dubious conscripts is not advisable. Why? Because people trust successful mentors with solid track records.

**Disgruntled employees:** These are often the best mentees and prospective entrepreneurs. They have the experience, assuming they are going into business in the field they left. They have the drive to succeed because they have something to prove. And what they may be lacking is the specific "know how." These mentees are often the most appreciative.

---

* Your **Business Model** is your gameplan for turning a profit, how you operate, what you sell/promote and who your target market might be. It's a snapshot of your business that acts as your comprehensive 'how to' guide and can also be presented to funders and investors.

† Your **Value Proposition** is defined as a statement that best and clearly summarizes why a customer would choose your product or service, and what benefits they derive from dealing with you.

**Non entrepreneurs:** This category includes inventors, government ex-employees, academia, and others who have depth in non-business environments, recognize their business gaps, and might be prepared to listen, learn, and work closely with an advisor.

**Shiny coin on the road:** The vacillator. Every shiny coin on the road is a distraction. A shifting focus is par for the course. The most difficult task for the mentor is to help eliminate the 'fluff' ideas, especially the ones that are difficult to realize, very costly (beyond the mentee's means), or demanding of a large and inordinate number of stakeholders brought to the table (permits, joint venture partners, regulatory bodies and other impeding parties). Once that arduous work is completed, there is generally a pathway cleared for a mentoring/mentee relationship. Enthusiasm is rarely lacking, but it can be an arduous journey.

## The Mentee Is the Flip Side of the Mentoring Process

*I've learned that people will forget what you said, people will forget what you did, but people will never forget how you made them feel.*
—Maya Angelou

Since every relationship takes two (or more) participants, it is vital for the mentor to understand as much as they can about the mentee prior to the start of the mentoring dance. That implies the use of a **Core Screening Document** to be completed by the mentee.

The key components of this document should include the following questions.

1. What is your business idea?
2. Are you already in business, or is this a startup?
3. Where did this idea come from? How was it born?
4. Why do you think it will succeed?
5. Do you think this has longevity/staying power, not a fad? Why do you think so?
6. How much homework/research have you done?

7. Have you identified your potential competitors? If so, how is what you are proposing different?

8. Have you completed a draft-only Business Plan?

9. Have you completed a preliminary Profit and Loss Statement?

10. Are your startup/launch costs identified? Guesstimated?

11. What is your Value Proposition? Why should anyone deal with you?

12. Have you identified the potential risks involved? Financial? Personal?

13. Do you have sufficient net worth to fund a portion of the initiative?

14. Have you had anybody review your idea, as a sounding board? If yes, what did they say?

15. What is your intended timing to bring your business on-stream?

16. Is this initiative time-sensitive? Season-sensitive?

# Are You Ready to Be a Mentee? Getting Into a Mentee's Head

*Spoon feeding, in the long run, teaches us nothing but the shape of the spoon.*

—E.M. Forster

The second part of prescreening the mentee is determining how robust they might be as entrepreneurs. A mentee whose "makeup" is geared toward fulfilling their business goals is far easier to work with than someone who is only giving entrepreneurship a glancing thought. Avoid the bored tire kicker.

Getting "inside the mentee's head" is an important part of prescreening mentorship participants.

"Getting your arms around" your prospective mentee participant is achieved by getting the following self-assessment completed by the candidate. It will tell you a great deal of who you are going to be dealing with, and best identify any gaps you may have to address.

What drives the mentee? The character of the entrepreneur is important. Entrepreneurship is about the character and willpower to succeed. It is a balance between "want" and "need," "money" and "fun," and "celebration" and "frustration."

The mentor's reputation is built on success. Catering to those whose interests and commitments are not "in the game" will simply negatively impact on the mentor's success batting average.

Here is an **Entrepreneur Self-Assessment Checklist** to help measure the mentee's entrepreneurial willpower and strength of character.

| *Getting Into a Mentee's Head* | *Yes? No? Do We Need to Talk About This?* |
| --- | --- |
| Are you hard-working? | |
| Do you stay focused on a project or task you are working on? | |
| Do you have a spirit of adventure? | |
| Do you have experience in the type of business you want to create? | |

(Continued)

| Getting Into a Mentee's Head | Yes? No? Do We Need to Talk About This? |
| --- | --- |
| Do you work well by yourself? | |
| Are you persistent? Stubborn? | |
| Do you get along well with others? | |
| Are you a risk taker? Calculated risk taker? Cautious and conservative? | |
| When you decide to do something, do you need to finish it? | |
| When you begin a task, do you set out goals? Steps to succeed? | |
| Do you tackle and solve problems? | |
| When people tell you it can't be done, do you still find a way to do it? | |
| Do you get personal satisfaction doing and completing a good job? | |
| Do you consider yourself a leader, or a follower? | |
| Do you need others to tell you that you are doing a good job? | |
| Do you avoid difficult or confrontational situations? | |
| Are you a good "loser" or a sore "loser" in competitive situations? | |
| Do you often seek advice from people? If no, are you open to it? | |
| How do you deal with others' input when you get negative feedback from someone? Do you get defensive? Angry? Upset? Are you grateful? | |
| Do you often act on other peoples' advice, counsel, or observations? | |
| Do you feel good about yourself? | |
| Do you like being in charge of other people? | |
| Do you enjoy working on projects that take a while to complete? | |
| Have your parents, grandparents, or close friends been in business? Has any of that rubbed off on you? | |

(Continued)

| Getting Into a Mentee's Head | Yes? No? Do We Need to Talk About This? |
|---|---|
| Do you usually come up with more than one solution to a problem? | |
| Do you find it easy to get others to do something for you? | |
| Are you an organized person? | |
| Are you constantly thinking of new ideas? Projects? | |
| Do you like to take care of details? | |
| Do you get bored easily? | |
| What rates higher; personal satisfaction or money? Why? | |
| Do you enjoy socializing, and meeting people? | |
| Any issues working long hours? Holidays? | |
| Do you believe in "good luck," or creating your own luck? | |
| Do you take rejection personally? | |
| Do you wake up happy most of the time? | |
| When you get an idea stuck in your head, do you constantly play it over and over? | |
| Do you believe entrepreneurship needs to be a huge risk? | |
| Can you accept failure without admitting defeat? | |
| Do you learn from your mistakes? | |
| How quickly do problems frustrate you? | |
| Do you "play well with others?"? | |
| Do you find change difficult, fun or challenging? | |
| Do you believe that "it's tough to make a living when all I do is work?" | |
| Are you a good listener? | |
| How important is position in the community for you? | |
| Do you learn from others, including strangers? | |

*(Continued)*

| *Getting Into a Mentee's Head* | *Yes? No? Do We Need to Talk About This?* |
|---|---|
| If someone gives you advice you don't believe, do you keep looking until someone agrees with you? | |
| What are the top five reasons you want to be in business? | |
| What are the top five things that can help you succeed? | |
| What are the top five things that can stop you from succeeding, and what can you do about them? | |
| Why do you think your business will succeed? | |

Once the mentee has had an opportunity to thoughtfully complete this backgrounder document, there should be time set aside for the mentor and mentor to discuss the content. Reproach and admonishments have no place in the interaction.

# What Mentees Should Do

- Before entering into a mentoring relationship, the mentee must know what they want, perhaps not all the intricate details, but certainly the scope of what their entrepreneurial vision might deliver.

- The general rule of thumb is that the mentor's advice is in your best interests. Unless proven otherwise, this doctrine forms the core of the relationship.

- Why did you undertake mentoring? The mentee needs to prepare a list of what they expect from mentoring, and what experience and expertise they are looking for in a mentor. Be specific. "I need help" is not specific.

- Generating a profile of the ideal mentor is helpful. It's like 'business dating'.

- Remain proactive. While you are sharing the reigns of the program, it is your desire that needs to drive it.

- The mentor will only work as hard as you challenge them.

- "If you don't ask, you don't get." Query the mentor on anything that you feel needs some objective and expert insight.

- Check your ego at the door. There is no room for extraneous defensiveness. Deal with the facts.

- Your role includes you providing feedback to the mentor on everything from what advice they offer to their style of mentoring. Communication between you both needs to be compatible.

- Remember that mentoring is an ongoing process of "baby steps." While there occasionally will be breakthrough "aha moments," the mainstay of the process is a steady trek forward. Don't get discouraged at the progress.

- Show your appreciation toward the mentor and you will get it back in return.

- Use the mentor as a sounding board, and do not hold back on your ideas.

- Story-telling, relaying past experiences, and role-playing are key tools in the mentor's toolbox. Go with them. Learn from them.
- Pay attention to how the mentor thinks and works out responses to your questions. Ask how they arrive at their responses. Learn strategic thinking from them.
- Perfectionism seldom exists. Accept that you will be somewhat less so, as will the mentor.
- Mentorship takes time. Find a way to balance your time availability, and do not shortchange family and friends in the process.
- Share what you have learned with others in the process. Networking with your peers yields opportunities.
- Take responsibility for the reward as well as the imperfections and shortcomings. Mentoring is a frail artform at best.
- Assume responsibility for the outcomes.
- **Use any number of viable resources to actually find a mentor.**
  - Business networking events such as Chamber soirees.
  - Conferences.
  - Referrals from trusted sources such as your accountant, banker, financial planner, or lawyer.
  - Social media searches (Google, Twitter, LinkedIn).
  - Entrepreneur "hotspots" such as business incubators/open workspace facilities.
  - SCORE (www.score.org/), the 11,000-plus-strong volunteer organization dedicated to helping individuals plan, start, and run their business. SCORE is just one example. There are others as you will find when you do some homework.
  - Indirect competitor referrals, that is, from those in the same industry as you but not direct competitors.

# What Mentees Should NOT Do

- Don't expect miracles, especially the overnight kind. Mentoring is a journey, not a race.
- Never expect the mentor to do what you should be doing. The mentor's role is distinctly not that hands-on, and you asking them to carry out your tasks such as market research or financial forecasting means that you are not learning self-reliance.
- Problems will arise, and that is a given. Don't bottle them up. Talk them out.
- You have a comfort zone. While not necessarily hiding in safety, be cautious about wandering too far outside your happy place.
- Decision-making is ultimately your responsibility. The mentor can advise, counsel, explain, and defend, but don't expect them to make the final decisions.
- Don't take criticism personally. While constructive criticism is one of those deflating and destructive oxymorons, it's not a reflection on you. Tough it out.
- Don't ask the mentor what you should do. Instead, work it out together. Take the lead.
- If it becomes clear that you and the mentor are operating at different levels, like a parent-child relationship, address it, fix it, or find another mentor. Do not try to fit into any relationship that is lopsided. Walk away if you cannot fix it. Some relationships are not worth salvaging.
- Avoid family and friends acting as mentors. Any feedback you get will most likely be of little use to you, or simply misleading. Your mother will always blindly agree with you, your friends may be jealous of you, and so it goes. Think of possible damaged personal relationships, skewed advice, and very stressful family Christmas dinners and birthday parties. All ugly.
- There are boundaries in the working relationship, as has been explained. Avoid stomping on those guidelines by

borrowing money from the mentor, developing a far-too-close friendship, or any other such activity that basically discards the norms of mentoring.

- A mentor may have experience in your sector, which is good. However, there may also be a conflict of interest, which is far less good. Find out before you take on the mentor.

# Beware the Toxic Mentor!

*With bad mentors, it's better to break up than to make up.*

—Jared Sandberg

Toxic mentors don't really see themselves as toxic. In fact, they usually exude overconfidence and know-it-all arrogance that they mistake as doling out advice, when, in fact, they are short on viable counsel and heavy on pomposity.

Mentees need to be cognizant of this mentoring trap before it adversely impacts their belief in mentorship, and the army of great mentors plying their trade.

## How Do You Recognize a Toxic Mentor? Here Are the Not-Too-Subtle Tell-Tale Signs

- Criticism becomes a power trip for them and is a tool they employ too easily and far too frequently.
- Belittling you, personally, and/or your initiative for which you are seeking mentoring help.
- Can make you feel guilty for just about anything, thereby undermining you and weakening your resolve. It's simply demeaning.
- Creates unwarranted discomfort between you both, but you are not quite certain why, or what the source of the friction might be.
- Encouragement is not part of the toxic mentor's toolbox.
- Trying to set a regular meeting schedule may be a challenge. The toxic mentor's time is inevitably much, much more valuable than yours.
- Listening to the mentee is replaced by the toxic mentor talking, sometimes incessantly. They pay little heed to what the mentee says. They like listening to themselves talk.
- Never admitting they are wrong or simply do not know.

- Boundaries are not well defined because, simply put, only the toxic mentor's boundaries are important. When these are one-sided parameters, the relationship becomes difficult.
- The toxic mentor often dishes out poor or bad advice that they stubbornly stand behind. The mentee recognizes that the advice or direction is incorrect. The result guarantees a clash of wills or business culture.
- Finally, the toxic mentor may feel that any NDA or Confidentiality Agreement does not apply to them. This breach of confidence is harmful to the mentee.

**When you see any of the above, don't try to fix the relationship. Walk away and find a mentor who should feel privileged to work with you. A good mentor should feel fortunate to work with a proactive, committed mentee. Hopefully, that's you.**

## Mentoring Adventures and Misadventures

My client owned a mall located in a rural area renowned for retirement homes and seniors' communities. There were few brand names retailers in the mall, more so locally owned clothing, giftware, and services catering to the core market.

Years before the demographics shifted to the baby boomers (and beyond), there was a public space dedicated to a games arcade. It was popular with the kids of the young families in the area, but now it was a revenue albatross to the mall owner.

My suggestion was to re-equip the arcade with retro games so very familiar to the new seniors' crowd; games such as Pac-Man, Pong, Asteroids, Missile Command, Parachute, Pinball, Galaxion, and others, all of which anybody over fifty might likely remember. Simple to use. Nostalgic. Corny, but memorable.

It was to include a coffee/tea bar and a small meeting area with comfortable seating.

This was to be an arcade for the new-old crowd. It was my idea to create revenues for the arcade and for the arcade to attract shoppers to the mall. All of the existing retailers agreed to fund the initiative.

It worked! The arcade became a hit and inspired the creation of competitive teams of seniors from within the region. Retail traffic increased dramatically.

Thinking outside the box is an inherent feature of mentoring.

# CHAPTER 4

# Gameplanning the Mentorship Journey

*A mentor empowers a person to see a possible future and believe it can be obtained.*

—Shawn Hitchcock

## The Mentorship Relationship-Building Gameplan

There is a symbiosis created between the mentor and the mentee in a mentoring relationship. This coaction between parties employs a proven, effective process/methodology.

Mentorship is comprised of a sequential series of steps/stages. Having used and fine-tuned the process, the phases fleshed out below represent the foundation of all my mentoring activity. It works.

## Where, How, and Why Mentees Seek Out Mentors

*In learning you will teach, and in teaching you will learn.*

—Phil Collins

It's time to turn the tables and find out why mentees seek out mentors, how they even find them, how they prepare for the mentoring, and what they expect from the exercise.

**Do you even need a mentor?** Here are a number of reasons for the mentee to pursue mentorship.

- Seek out someone who has specialized knowledge and experience within your chosen sector
- A qualified sounding board to bounce your ideas off, and someone unafraid to offer constructive advice
- Possibly increase your knowledge, market perspective, or the inner workings of your business by looking from the outside in
- An arms-length third party to acknowledge your efforts and hopefully heap praise on you
- Everybody in business needs a friend, and a mentor can fulfill that role. Friends connect friends to the right people and share their network
- Having someone impartial look at your idea/plans from a thirty-thousand-foot view can best review your proposed or existing venture or business, and comment on opportunities or challenges you might be oblivious to

The mentee has the opportunity to screen the mentor as well with a series of pointed questions. In fact, it is the mentees responsibility to query until they are satisfied that the person (mentor) whom they will be opening up to is the right matchup for them.

Prepare a profile of your ideal mentor; what their experience might be; age and style; background; reputation; and credibility. Check them out. Ask around. Ask for references.

Without making it all appear to be an interrogation, the mentee's questions to the mentor can be divided into several categories.

### Personal

- *What prompted you to become a mentor?*
- *Has it been a personally rewarding experience for you?*
- *What is your availability of time to work with me?*
- *What makes you a successful mentor?*
- *What skills and personal features do you have that make you an effective mentor?*
- *What inspires you?*

## Professional

- *What is your experience in my sector?*
- *What is your success rate?*
- *Can you give me a few examples of your mentoring stories? The best? The worst?*
- *Are there people or companies in your network that you can and would refer to me to help me build my business?*
- *How many mentoring assignments do you currently have? How many do you juggle at any one time, and still have the time to focus on each one?*
- *If you were me, would you take on this initiative?*
- *How do you assure confidentiality of what we talk about?*

## Style and Communications

- *How would you describe your communication skills?*
- *When you arrive at an impasse with the mentee, how do you handle it?*
- *Do you expect all your recommendations to be acted on?*
- *How often should we meet?*
- *How do you prefer meeting? Online? Face-to-face?*
- *Do you normally give me "homework" to prepare for each meeting?*

Once you have fine-tuned your mentoring needs and drafted your goals and expectations, how do you find a mentor to work with?

- There may be people within your own network who would be suitable candidates. This could include more experienced business associates and professionals.
- Consider approaching people you admire. You will find successful people are often keen to 'give back', or 'pay it forward'.
- Network at events, conferences, in fact, just about everywhere there is a gathering.

- Online mentoring matchup services are available, but need careful screening on your part. There are many, many wannabes, professed instant-gratification gurus, and snake oil salespeople. Do your homework. Ask for references. Be guarded before you divulge proprietary information.
- Join networking organizations and associations, and become a proactive member.
- Create an elevator pitch that you can use within your networking activities, and see who shows an interest.
- Join industry associations geared to your sector. Attend industry meetings and shop around.
- Don't be shy. Request meetings with candidates you think might be suitable and willing. If not, ask for referrals.

Before you leap, mutually agree to a "honeymoon period" of working together to see the fit, chemistry, and shared vision. This is an important precursor to smooth any wrinkles that might crop up between you later on.

## Preliminary Meeting Online or Face-to-Face

This opening gambit sets the framework for all the mentoring sessions that will follow. It is also an opportunity for each party to, hopefully, begin to build a comfort zone around the process, which will allow an open dialog and an honest and ongoing exchange of information.

The mentor needs to "match" the mentee in style, level of enthusiasm, attitude, and even body language that will help generate naturalness on the part of the mentee.

This even includes attire. If the mentee wears jeans and a sports shirt, the mentor should copy that informality. It creates a club-like working atmosphere.

This preliminary meet should not be done by e-mail or other electronic means. Each party must be able to read the signals that only face-to-face and body language can provide.

Key phrases the mentor can use:

- *"Let me tell you a little about myself. You should know who you are letting into your confidence."*
- *"Any questions about me?"*
- *"We'll set out the guidelines, timing, goals, and expectations soon, but first, tell me about your business, what needs you have and how you think I can help."*
- *"I am curious, where did this idea come from?"*
- *"How long have you been working on this?"*
- *"Why do you think it will succeed? Explain it to me as if I have a checkbook in my hands."*
- *"What is the best way for us to meet? Online Zoom or Face-to-Face?"*

Getting the mentoring process started triggers a number of sensitivities and insecurities on the part of the mentee, especially if this is their first experience. In many cases, the mentee looks upon the mentor as some deity who will solve their problems, deliver opportunities to them, assure that there is no pain or undue hardship inflicted on their initiative, and teach them how to deal with the host of "nasties" that competition and fussy markets can represent. In this startup mentoring process, the mentor is too often seen as a God. This image needs to be dispelled to avoid mentee disappointment.

There is also the expectation that the mentor will do everything when, in fact, the mentor is the tour guide, pointing out highlights and guiding the mentorship tour. The actual work like market research, numbers crunching, planning, marketing, and other strategic tasks are the prevue of the mentee, not the mentor.

This calls for the setting of rules and guidelines at a very early stage in the process. Defining the roles and responsibilities is of foremost importance. Everyone needs to know their place in the chain.

## Agreement Between Both Parties

1. You go into this relationship as "relative" equals, each bringing strengths, knowledge, and enthusiasm to the table. Outwardly, the mentor is no better than the mentee, and vice versa. The key word here is "relative" because, in the process, the mentor is always the "sage" and the mentee is always the "protégé." Each player recognizes and respects their place in the hierarchy.

2. Nothing that is offered by the mentor is cast in concrete. The mentee is allowed and actually encouraged to question. That is part of the learning curve. Sometimes both parties need to agree to disagree.

3. Neither party's time is more valuable than the others' time. Both need to be mindful of what busy schedules people have.

4. There are boundaries and etiquette around the mentorship process. However, even at the very early stage, the mentee needs to understand that this is a structured process and not a free-for-all.

5. Honesty builds trust. Everything either party says and does needs to be transparent and truthful.

6. Agree that everything disclosed is to remain confidential.

Aside from the above, **there are some critical foundational and functional cornerstones. This is called the 'honeymoon stage' that the mentor needs to institute quickly before moving on to the preliminary mentorship steps.**

- For the mentor, there is some urgency in establishing trust with the mentee participant. Failing that, the process goes nowhere except into obscurity.
- Cultivate a strong connection through personal communication.
- Zero in on the mentee's needs, challenges, and aspirations.
- Why is the mentee pursuing the mentorship journey? Find out.
- Be clear that you intend to ask the mentee to carry out "homework" after each session based on what was covered in

the get-together. The mentee needs to show they buy into the process. It's an important part of the mentoring.

- Set a timetable for regular meetings, and how those meetings will happen (Zoom, face-to-face, other). It needs to be something everyone can adhere to, and allow the mentee to complete any "homework" assignments.
- Every relationship has boundaries, etiquette that needs to be observed, and dos and don'ts. Use the first meeting to discuss these. (*Note: this book has a complete chapter on mentoring etiquette.*)
- Emphasize that the relationship needs to not only be fruitful and productive but also comfortable.
- Explain that you intend to be both a cheerleader/motivator celebrating the mentee's progress and achievement, and also the "devil's advocate" when the situation warrants.
- Mentees in the birthing of a project or initiative can be scattered and "all over the map." Keeping the mentee organized is key, and the mentee should know the mentor intends to carry out this role.
- Explain the dilemma of "mentoring burnout," which can rear up for any number of reasons. Both parties should remain cognizant of dwindling interest and focus.
- Cover the need for confidentiality. This will help with the mentee's comfort level.
- Discuss personal and career backgrounds that you may both have in common.
- The mentor should share stories about his mentoring experiences, particularly those that may be relevant to the mentee's journey at hand.
- State why each of you is doing what you're doing. This helps seal the relationship.
- Build a box around the mentee's goals and aspirations. That is your starting point.
- The mentor could also talk about the "dance" of mentoring, that is the highs and lows experienced by the mentee. Prepare the mentee to expect hiccups along the way.

- Start to set up a timeline and gameplan to follow so that both parties can buy into it.
- The mentor needs to encourage the mentee to open up and talk.
- The mentor needs to listen intently.
- The mentor can ask the mentee to quantify their vision for the mentoring relationship, expectations, and the added value they expect from mentorship.

# The Core Screening Process

This screening process is similar to the content of a brief Executive Overview.* It also helps the mentor and mentee affirm the foundation of their initiative, and possibly identify any gaps in the model.

Key phrases the mentor can use:

- *"This screening process helps me get my arms around your initiative so that the mentoring process can be more effective."*
- *"This will help shape how we work together."*
- *"Everything we talk about is held in the strictest confidence."*
- *"Any questions that you do not want to respond to?" "Why or why not?"*

### Presenting the Entrepreneurs' Self-Assessment Checklist

Why is this important? The checklist (*See "Is the Mentee Entrepreneur Ready?"*) provides the mentee with a collection of features that exemplify the profile of a businessperson. At the same time, it quickly and painlessly zeroes in on any gaps or shortcomings the mentee may have in their own critical skillsets and mindset. This allows the mentee to consider any changes they need to institute.

The mentor is also given an inside track to what makes the mentee "tick." That will prove to be invaluable in planning and delivering the mentorship program.

Key phrases the mentor can use:

- *I actually complete one of these regularly. It tells me how I myself am doing as an entrepreneur, and if there is anything not quite working for me.*

---

* An Executive Overview is generally the first section of a Business Plan. It is characterized by the key points of your plan and how you propose to achieve results for your business. It is a "speed read" of what you propose, and what you need.

- *This checklist will give me a snapshot of you as an entrepreneur. It will help set the tone of our working together.*
- *Please fill this in honestly. This checklist is only between you and me.*
- *Think about any response you fill in as 'maybe' or 'no'. These might be issues that we need to talk about.*

## Reviewing the Entrepreneurs' Self-Assessment Checklist Together

The opportunity to review the checklist (previously completed by the mentee) together is an exercise in building trust and communication.

In this stage, it is best to allow the mentee to take the leading role in discussing their responses.

Key phrases the mentor can use:

- *"Thank you for taking the time to do this."*
- *"Rest assured this is treated as highly confidential."*
- *"Any line items you particularly had difficulty with?"*
- *"Most of this looks very encouraging, but there are a few vague spots. Can we talk about them?"*
- *"Did you identify any glaring gaps or problem areas we need to address?"*

## Laying Down the Mentorship Ground Rules

If the mentoring process is to work, there are a number of ground rules, best referred to as structure and guidelines. This includes the etiquette of how to behave in the course of working closely together, that is, what is expected from each party. The mentee needs to understand and buy into these.

Further, there are a series of "dos and don'ts" that apply to both parties, and these should be reviewed and agreed upon. These have previously been identified in the "Etiquette" chapters herein.

When these ground rules/etiquette/dos and don'ts are presented and discussed, the framework for the mentorship will proceed with far fewer interruptions and interludes.

Key phrases the mentor can use:

- *"You may be aware of many of these mentoring protocols and guidelines that apply to each of us, but we should review them together."*
- *"Setting ground rules lets each of us know what is expected of us, what to do and not do, and how to get the most out of working together."*
- *"Structure and borders build a comfortable, workable relationship."*
- *"I am offering this up from experience in working with other mentees."*
- *"If any guidelines give either of us trouble along the way, we can certainly talk."*

## Setting Needs and Expectations

Here is where the details start to emerge. It is in the mentee's ballpark to deliver a concise recounting of what they feel they need to accomplish in order to move forward.

This applies equally to a newbie/start-up as it does for an established businessperson looking to grow, expand their products or services, acquire others, be acquired by others and dealing with new competitors who are leapfrogging them ... and the list of circumstances is almost endless.

For each challenge, the mentee should also prepare how they would undertake remedial action if left to their own devices. This will also provide the mentor with an insight to the mentee's frame of mind and decision-making process.

Key phrases the mentor can use:

- *"If these are your needs, and these accompanying items are the actions you would take, how exactly do you see this happening?"*
- *"Which of these items are the most important? Let's prioritize them."*

- *"We need to assume that anything you need that takes a bunch of people being brought to the table will take time."*
- *"Which do you consider the lowest hanging fruit?"*

## Defining the Mentor's Role

What does the mentee expect of you? Miracles, no doubt. Jumping over tall buildings? Certainly.

There is a process of aligning what the mentee wants (realistically) and needs (even more realistically) with what the mentor can deliver. And the sooner you align the stars, the greater the chances that your mentorship will be fruitful.

Make sure the mentee appreciates your experience and capabilities and recognizes your limitations. Unreasonable expectations should be put to rest quickly.

Key phrases the mentor can use:

- *"What do you expect to get out of this mentoring?"*
- *"What expectations do you have of me? How do you think I can help you?"*
- *"Have you had mentoring before? Was it successful? Tell me about it."*
- *If you were to design the perfect mentor, what would they be like?"*

## The Crucial Reality Check

Experience has taught me that most entrepreneurs want everything "yesterday." That could be because they are anxious to proceed, worried about looming competition, losing any kind of technical or competitive edge, or, worst case, because they are coming in on the tail end of an existing opportunity.

It is incumbent on the mentor to set expectations straight right from the get-go; nothing happens overnight; there will almost always be competition in the marketplace, so just focus on being better; and the mentee who wants to instantly own the world must learn to walk before they run.

The reality check can be perceived by the mentee that you do not have confidence in what they are doing, or do not have the "compassion" for instant-type success. Since neither is likely correct, the mentor needs to inflict the minimum of pain by being approachable.

Key phrases the mentor can use:

- *Interesting goals. What timeframes do you feel are realistic in reaching them? Is your timetable too aggressive or too relaxed? Please explain.*
- *In my experience, timing is always an issue. Too fast and you may be overlooking something, either an opportunity or a risk. Too slow and the lifespan of the opportunity can simply expire.*
- *Let's revisit the timelines. I need to get a clearer understanding of your expectations.*

## Deep Diving

Over the course of time, you and your charge will have numerous opportunities to dive into the details of the mentoring mandate, exactly what is the achievable end goal and the feasibility of the initiative.

Along the way, it will be the mentor's responsibility to determine how prepared the mentee is and offer assistance in determining the project's viability. The mentor should do this by proposing alternate research and homework for the mentee to carry out. (*See Appendixes for resources that the mentee can be directed to.*)

**The role of the mentor is not to do the work for the mentee, but to direct the mentee to the best resources to carry out the identified and necessary research and planning action items.**

Key phrases the mentor can use:

- *"How is your market research panning out? How much have you had a chance to do?"*
- *"What type of homework have you been able to do; web research, visit competitors, sign up for their newsletters; review their pricing policies and discounts; how they market themselves?"*

- *"Have you done any role modeling, that is, finding distant like-companies and interviewed them with a list of ten questions? If they were sitting across from you, what would you want to ask them?" Start with these.*

1. How did you start their business?
2. Are you profitable? How long did it take you to start operating profitably?
3. How did you find and secure your customers?
4. How risky was it to start your business?
5. How did you know you would succeed?
6. How much startup money did you need?
7. "What have you learned that I could apply to (or avoid in) my enterprise?"
8. "Have you identified any pitfalls you should have avoided?"
9. Did your competitors "come after you?" If so, how did you handle it?
10. How do you stay competitive?

### Setting Achievable Milestones and Timeline

It is critical to keep in mind that the milestones and timelines are "owned" by the mentee. **It is not so much what the mentor thinks, but what the mentee feels comfortable committing to.**

There may be extenuating circumstances impacting the mentee's progress or their ability to focus on achieving progress, such as family, financing, or health. These are normal life's imposing brake pedals.

However, it is the mentor's role to assess whether any delays are being caused by dwindling interest and motivation, in which case, this needs to be addressed with the mentee.

Once cast, the mentor needs to be highly cognizant of maintaining progress and moving forward on the agreed-upon milestones and timelines.

Projects that tread water are generally heading toward the graveyard of unfulfilled opportunities.

# Create a Mentorship Contract

*My job is not to be easy on people. My job is to take these great people we have and to push them and make them even better.*

—Steve Jobs

There is a distinct advantage in drafting and signing a mentorship contract. Each party recognizes and agrees as to what is expected, what each party's roles are, and how the mentorship progress is tracked.

This is a "moral contract." Very little here is enforceable by any legal means. However, once signed, it is binding as to the behavior, performance, and identified contributions of the mentor and mentee as they work in unison toward fulfilling the goals and objectives of the mentee.

**It is as much a personal statement of joint commitment as it is a contract.** Nevertheless, it can be the foundation of a working mentorship relationship and something that can be referred back to if things go awry.

*(Please note that this Contract Template has been filled in with hypothetical itemized examples. This will help the reader(s) understand the core function and intent of the Agreement.)*

## The Mentoring Contract Template

This contract is between **John Smith**, the Mentor, and **Lisa Duval**, the Mentee and is binding insofar as both parties have agreed to respect the terms and conditions as outlined herein.

This relationship has been entered for a period of **six months** commencing **January 14, 20XX.**

It is understood that the mentee has sought out the services of the mentor to facilitate with the following issues and challenges as identified by the mentee:

1. Business planning and the preparation of a business plan
2. Operational issues, how to run a business
3. How do I measure risk?

4. How can I research competition?

5. Steps I need to take to impress funders

Prior to the signing of this contract, the parties have taken sufficient time, as deemed by the signatories, to get to know each other, on a preliminary basis, are comfortable in entering into this relationship, and have discussed the desired outcome of the mentorship.

The mentorship is focused around the mentee's initiative as described briefly below.

> My ambition is to open a series of upscale clothing stores, using my training as a designer and artist. I have had some retail experience but little entrepreneurial training.

The mentee's short-term goals are prioritized as below.

1. Help me understand if this business makes sense.
2. Prepare a budget with me.
3. Introduce me to others who might be of help to me.
4. Design a brand and marketing plan together.
5. Introduce me to a couple of funders so I can gage their interest.

The mentee's long-term goals are prioritized as below.

1. Generate a Business Plan that I can follow.
2. Find a location for the flagship store.
3. Find manufacturers that can make my product.
4. Get media attention for me and my brand.
5. Think about other locations, licensing, and expansion.

Where deemed feasible, the parties agree to target the following milestones as deemed achievable and realistic. These are the best guestimates and open to alterations or modifications during the mentorship process.

1. Meeting every three weeks
2. Market and competition research carried out within two months

3. Speaking with others in the industry within three to four months
4. Agreeing on a realistic budget and forecast within four months
5. Developing a series of action plan items within five months

The mentee represents that they are free and clear of any encumbrances or that they have dealt with regarding their products, services, IP, licensing, certification, or other constraints that may have an impact upon the success of the business.

To facilitate an open and mutually beneficial relationship, each party has identified their strengths, experience, and relative expertise being brought to the process.

### Mentee

1. Clothing and fashion design
2. Graduate of the Western Institute of Design
3. Five years in clothing retail business
4. Three years working for a clothing production house
5. I feel I have a pretty strong commitment to seeing this through, if I can

### Mentor

1. Mentor experienced in startup and early-stage business ventures
2. Several years working in the fashion industry
3. Mentored a number of established industry-related businesses in the past
4. Availability in terms of allocating time to the client
5. Connections in the funding sector for new venture launches

Both parties will strive, on a best efforts basis, to govern themselves according to the following:

1. Communicate in an open, honest matter.
2. Meet regularly as mutually agreed to and through whatever means is convenient to both.
3. Be respectful of each other's time availability.

4. Discuss mentor feedback in an open manner, and, where necessary, agree to disagree without disrupting the overall mentoring process.
5. Be totally transparent in all matters.
6. Foster a positive attitude and working relationship.
7. Maintain strict confidentiality.
8. Review progress on a regular basis and mutually agree to any changes necessitated by the assessment. The following follow-up schedule has been agreed to, where the progress of the mentorship will be reviewed and discussed:
   * Every xx months, or
   * Review dates based on milestones achieved

Each party undertakes to be responsible for the following roles and will deliver the same, on a best efforts basis, to the levels acceptable by the other party.

---

**Mentee**
1. **Respect the schedule of mentoring sessions.**
2. **Give due consideration to the advice provided by the mentor.**
3. **Carry out the research, planning, and homework suggested by the mentor.**
4. **Seek out other sounding boards as suggested by the mentor.**
5. **Create a Business Plan and Marketing Plan.**

---

**Mentor**
1. **Provide mentoring services on a regularly scheduled basis.**
2. **Offer resources that are useful to the mentee.**
3. **Carry out due diligence on whatever the mentee proposes.**
4. **Act as "devil's advocate."**
5. **Deliver counsel in the best interest of the mentee.**

Both parties agree to the following tentative communications schedule:

---

**Meeting Details**
- **Frequency: Every 3 weeks**
- **Day and Time: Try for 3 PM mentoring sessions**
- **Scheduled Duration: 1.5 hours each**
- **Location and Digital Means: Zoom**
- **Meeting Cancelation Notices: One week**

---

In the course of the relationship, the mentor will attempt, where feasible, to introduce the mentee to contacts, other professionals, and other parties who may be of benefit to the mentee.

### *Other Terms and Conditions*

This Mentoring Contract, in whole or in part, will form the basis of a Mentoring Plan agreed to by both parties.

In the course of this process, the mentee may offer and the mentor will receive confidential information and documents including, but not limited to, Business Plans, budgets, market research, marketing strategies, pricing and policies, Intellectual Property, and any other information that sharing with outside third parties may result in damages to the mentee. Strict confidentiality will be maintained by the mentor, unless permission to share is granted in writing by the mentee.

The mentor shall not be deemed an employee of the mentee's company.

Any fee structures that may be agreed upon shall be strictly between the parties and shall be deemed as consulting fees.

Either party has the right to terminate this contract with thirty days' notice and without cause. Upon termination, all hard copy and digital documentation shared by the mentee to the mentor shall be returned, and confidentiality shall survive for 12 months following the termination date.

Contact information for both parties is as follows:

**Mentee**
- **Cellphone: 555-861-7896**
- **Fax: Nil**
- **E-mail: mentee@gmail.com**
- **Address: 14 Terrace Drive, NY**

**Mentor**
- **Cellphone: 555-665-9888**
- **Fax: Nil**
- **E-mail: mentor@gmail.com**
- **Address: not available**

## Liability

The mentor shall not be held liable for any advice, counsel, or action recommended to the mentee where the mentee acts upon said information.

The mentor shall not be held liable for any advice, counsel, or action recommended to the mentee where the mentee does not act upon said information and thereby incurs losses or damages.

The mentee agrees to engage, on their own accord and at their own expense, any third party to assess any recommendations offered by the mentor. In these instances, the breach of confidentiality to third parties shall not apply.

Nothing in this contract is intended or shall be deemed to constitute a partnership or joint venture of any kind between the parties.

Any person who is not a party to this contract shall not have any rights enshrined in this contract.

This contract is duly signed and accepted by both parties on (date) **January 5, 20XX** at (location) **New York, New York.**

_____          _____

Mentor                                                              Mentee

# Time for a SWOT Analysis (Strengths, Weaknesses, Opportunities, Threats)

Delivering quantifiable results is a cornerstone of mentorship. It is vital to work together to carry out an analysis of the mentoring effort, that is, what was planned versus what was or is in the process of being realized. This is similar to a financial budget; what was budgeted versus what was expensed.

Key phrases the mentor can use:

- *"Being an outsider looking in, I might be able to inject more objective strategies and issues than you."*
- *Strengths: "What personal strengths and skills have you been able to bring to the table?" "Why do you think this initiative is as strong, stronger, or weaker than when you launched it?"*
- *Weaknesses: "We all know every initiative has weaknesses. Have you identified any that we need to address, ones that are or can have an impact on getting things done?"*
- *Opportunities: "Your goals have always striven to seizing opportunities, but in the course of your research and work, have you identified new, secondary, or offshoot opportunities? Let's talk about them and see how we might help make them happen or if they are logical to be pursued. Do these other opportunities distract you from your original primary business focus?"*
- *Threats: "Risks are the fiends of business. Let's address dealing with the ones you have control over, such as competition, and then cover the ones where you have little or no control, such as the economy."*

## Setting Mentoring Get-Togethers

Keeping mentoring sessions on some kind of regular basis helps maintain the momentum of the process, and encourages the mentee to complete any "homework" they may have been assigned, or research and market and target audience outreach.

It is the mentee who sets the timing based on their time availability, and the mentor who works to adhere to the agreed-upon schedule.

While there is always a bit of flexibility, especially when 'life might get in the way', the overall frequency of get-togethers should be reasonably steady and regular.

Key phrases the mentor can use:

- *I will try to make myself available to meet your proposed mentoring timing.*
- *It is your schedule and availability that can set the timing of our sessions. What do you suggest?*
- *Is the initiative you are working on time-sensitive?*

# Role Playing

Role-playing tends to be one of my favorite mentoring tools. Perhaps it's the theatrics in me. Regardless, it is highly effective in casting events, issues, problems, and challenges into a real-life framework.

One such example is when a mentee is about to seek out funding. The mentor takes on the role of a funding manager, pummeling with "devil's advocate type" questions, such as these to better prepare the mentee for any pending presentations or meetings.

Key phrases the mentor can use:

- *"Explain your business model to me like I was a first grader."*
- *"Who will buy from you? Why do you think so?"*
- *"Why should the investor/bank fund you?"*
- *"Tell me how you will succeed, without any rose-colored glasses."*
- *"I don't really understand your budget numbers. Walk me through them."*

The idea is to make the mentee think and also to learn how to be quick on their feet, ready for any intrusive questioning.

Another example may be to query any stats that the mentee may be embracing. That could include market share sought, target demographics, market size and trends, competition numbers, and other key data that would impact the mentee's venture. Always push the mentee to back up any statements with traceable and timely sources. Outdated data or old market information is damaging to the mentee's cause.

## The Funnel Effect

The mentor's focus needs to be pinpoint precision and unwavering. Unfortunately, the mentee's ideas and planning may be scattered like buckshot. That's just the way a mentee's energy often fires.

There is a technique called "**Funneling Down**" which the mentor needs to master. It implies taking a large number of items as generated by the mentee and running them through a funnel; more like a meat grinder.

The idea is to narrow down the mentee's focus and work to assure certain items are dealt with in a priority sequence. Anything less broadens the mentorship efforts until little gets done as the mentee chases distractions.

Key phrases the mentor can use:

- *Everything is great, but just too liquid. Let's focus down on the most pressing stuff.*
- *Let's start with what we can deal with today, and leave the rest for later.*
- *I don't think we should drop the ball on what we have been talking about, so let's backburner everything except this.*

# Storytelling

Storytelling implies offering up (but done confidentially) situations you have found yourself in or experienced with other clients, that relate specifically to the current mentoring mandate.

Storytelling can consist of positive experiences, in which you would also talk about how the topic or event was resolved. This relays a learning experience for the mentee, but taught by example.

The opposite is also true. Discussing failures provides a learning opportunity for the mentee, a lesson in avoiding the quicksand.

In many cases, a modicum of humor is an excellent groundbreaker for the discussion.

And if you don't have the stories to tell, make them up, as long as they fit the situations at hand. Nobody will know, and the mentee will not be the wiser for it. Welcome to "elastic ethics."

Key phrases the mentor can use:

- *What you are running into here happened to me a while back. Here is how it got resolved without bringing down my freshly constructed walls.*
- *This real-life story might help us find a solution.*
- *Sometimes hands-on experience is a great teacher. Here's an example.*

# Never Saying "No"

Mentors who are overworked or disinterested in the nature of the mentee's goals and needs are very prone to say "no," as in "this can't work" or "that doesn't make good sense."

Saying "no" is just too easy. Instead, if the mentor is truly and adamantly taking issue with something, they should find a workaround. There's always another perspective to employ.

Key phrases the mentor can use:

- *My first impulse is to say 'no', but that is unfair. Let's find a way to make sense of this.*
- *I never say 'no', but I sometimes offer up alternate avenues and pathways for you to consider.*

# Positive Psychology

As you can detect, herein and throughout this book, mentoring is 50 percent counsel and training and 50 percent psychology, the science of mind and behavior.

"Positive psychology" focuses on what is working well, what interactions can represent project building blocks, and how to avoid the kind of negativity that halts the process.

Entrepreneurship is also a process of change, often quite a dramatic experience for the mentee. Change meets resistance. The entrepreneur who does what they have always done will realize the same results, and without being open to change, that is a process of treading water. Neither scenario is workable.

Key phrases the mentor can use:

- *What, if anything, needs to change in your attitude and mindset to make you a better entrepreneur?*
- *Do you accept or resist change? Explain.*
- *Does your business opportunity demand that you change how you best deal with morals, scruples, dealing with people, decision-making, business 'right and wrong' ethics, and personal values?*

# Managing the Mentor's Load of Mentees

Managing mentees can equate to herding feral cats. Almost every mentee will want your attention when it fits their schedule, and often when it puts you into a conflict with other appointments.

It is crucial for the mentee to understand that you are not a limitless, "open twenty-four hour" resource. There are limits to be respected.

There are basically three major areas the mentor needs to learn to juggle.

1. **Managing a client load:** Taking on too many mentees will limit the time you have to spend with each, and will naturally reduce the quality of all your programs. Determine what your workload limits are, remembering that while all efforts are made to schedule regular sessions, the mentoring process does not necessarily travel in a straight line.

2. **Disruptive scheduling:** Mentees' cancelations and rebooking of sessions can create havoc in your agenda. Prepare for coping by allocating certain hours in the day for mentoring, and try to maintain that schedule of availability.

3. **Dealing with mentee personal issues:** Avoid getting involved in the personal goings-on of your mentees. As much as you might like to help, involvement will damage your image of impartiality, and ravenously eat your time.

Key phrases the mentor can use:

- *Client load: I will gladly take you on for mentoring as soon as my portfolio of mentees levels out.*
- *Scheduling: While my mentoring sessions schedule is somewhat flexible, I cannot always reschedule based only on your availability.*
- *Mentees getting personal: I understand what you are going through. Perhaps a break in the mentoring process is worthwhile while you deal with those issues.*

# Completing the Mentoring Process

All things come to an end. Hopefully, your mentorship has yielded results for the mentee, both quantitatively and qualitatively.

Together you should determine when the end has been reached, defined as the mentee acting independently without your involvement, identified goalposts met or exceeded, and the mentor recognizing when they are not needed anymore.

Follow-up x months after the completion of the program is a viable timeframe to determine mentorship deliverables and the success of your program.

A task for the mentee:

- *Generate a satisfaction survey.*
  - *Do you feel the mentoring program has been successful for you? Please explain.*
  - *Has the mentoring changed the course of your initiative? Please explain.*
  - *Was the mentor's style in line with your own? Did this make it easier? Yes or no? Please explain.*
  - *Did the program deliver what you had expected? Please list five areas that the mentoring has made a difference, and explain each.*
  - *Was the mentoring also like a training program for you? Learned more about business/entrepreneurship? Please explain.*
  - *What did you like most about the program?*
  - *What did you like least about the program?*

## Build on Your Successes

When the mentor has succeeded with a mentee, it is worthy of noting this accomplishment.

Feel free to approach the mentee and ask permission to use them as a reference and a quote in your own website or resume.

Key phrases the mentor can use:

- *The success we had working together is noteworthy. If I maintain total confidentiality, can I have your permission to discuss the mentorship so that others may appreciate how this program delivers?*

## How the Mentee Gauges Success

*If you want to lift yourself up, lift up someone else.*
—Booker T. Washington

When would the mentee consider a mentorship engagement a success?

1. You are able to open up and feel safe in their presence.
2. You feel comfortable going to the mentor when you are facing a problem.
3. There is open communication without fear or concern about retribution.
4. The conversation is about you, the mentee, and not about the mentor.
5. Feedback offered is noncritical.
6. The relationship between the mentor and mentee has boundaries that you can accept and live within.
7. The mentor is being sought to help or even fix mistakes, and does so.
8. You let go when you both feel it's time to let go.
9. The two of you stay in touch and there is continuous follow-up, with contact becoming less frequent over time.

The mentee's progress can be tracked with successive reports and status snapshots. This chapter is about *The Mentee Report Card.*

The purpose of this *Mentee Report Card* is to score the results of the mentor-mentee journey from the mentee's qualitative vantage point; the progress and the outcome(s). It is intended as an "end of term" report when the mentee is ready to move on.

For each line item, score "F" (failure or lacking), G = good, VG = very good, or E = excellent.

## *The Mentee Report Card: Assessing the Mentorship Experience*

| Achieved? | Score? |
|---|---|
| Goals and business objectives were clearly defined. | |
| Achievable milestones were set and mutually agreed to. | |
| Mentoring sessions generally exhibited progress toward defined goals. | |
| Progress over the course of the mentoring was quantifiable. | |
| Results were materialized within the expected timeframe. | |
| Mutual agreement that the mentoring has served its purpose. | |
| Follow up in 3, 6, and 12 months was agreed to. | |
| Notes: | |

## Learning Is a Two-Way Street. Let's Take This One Step Farther

This *Mentor Report Card* would provide the mentor with feedback on their mentoring style and how well the process was received and appreciated by the mentee.

## How Well Did the Mentor Succeed in the Opinion of the Mentee?

## *The Mentee Report Card: Assessing the Mentor*

| Achieved? | Score? |
|---|---|
| Trust established in the relationship. | |
| Definable and achievable goals were set together. | |
| Positive and motivating mentoring sessions. | |
| Mentor shared control of the sessions. | |
| Progress was realized. | |
| Goals were met and the mentorship program fulfilled its objectives and ended. | |
| Follow up in 3, 6, and 12 months was carried out. | |
| Notes: | |

The mentorship goals can also be scrutinized. The "rule of thumb" applies the well-known **Smart Goals**[†] to gauge the success of a mentoring relationship. This is a useful ancillary exercise. It eliminates "pie in the sky" thinking.

- Were the goals **SPECIFIC**, as in readily definable?
- Could the goals be **MEASURED** using a relatable and reliable yardstick?
- Aiming high is fine, but were the goals **ACHIEVABLE** (and realistic)?
- Were the goals **RELEVANT** to the end results defined by the mentee?
- If there was a window of opportunity, was the **TIMELINE** met?

All of the above can be accomplished via survey or questionnaire, but preferably by face-to-face interview where both parties can speak openly and freely, with a high priority focus on the input from the mentee themselves.

**With all this post analysis completed and in hand, the mentor and mentee will have both learned from the experience. Hopefully, this knowledge base would serve them well as they move on to new relationships.**

## *Mentoring Adventures and Misadventures*

I had two young women mentees who intended to start an online artists co-operative and sales website. The ongoing conversation went something like this.

ME: "Tell me what you want to do."
THEM: "Sell artists work online."
ME: "Ever done this before?"
THEM: "No"

---

[†] www.smartsheet.com/blog/essential-guide-writing-smart-goals, https://asana.com/resources/smart-goals.

ME: "So how many artists have you got signed?"
THEM: "Two"
ME: "Have you got agreements with them? Commissions worked out?"
THEM: "We talked."
ME: "How many pieces can you launch with?"
THEM: "Five or six"
ME: "How much commission will you take?"
THEM: "Ten percent"
ME: "Really? Can you make any money with only 10 percent?"
THEM: "That's what you can tell us, right?"
ME: "How much money do you need to get started?"
THEM: "Yes"
ME: "Well, how much do you need?"
THEM: "Well … "
ME: "If I was the banker, how much would you ask me for?"
THEM: "Well … "
ME: "Have you started on a business plan?"
THEM: "We don't think we need one."
ME: "Budgets? Can you make any money at this?"
THEM: ??????????
ME: "Find someone who is already doing what you want to do, research everything about them, go speak with them, then come back to me if you are still serious about this, ok?"
THEM: ??????????

Miscommunication, insufficient ground rules set beyond several preliminary get-togethers, unreasonable expectations, little research done on their part, and on and on it went. I sent them away with a shopping list of what they needed to get done before we met again.

1. Why do you think this will succeed?
2. Show me what research you have done.
3. Who will buy from you, and why? Prove it.
4. Who is your competition? What makes you different?
5. How much money do you need?

This was early in my mentoring work and taught me some important lessons in pre screening, preparation, and defining the roles of both the mentor and the mentee. Prescreen. Assume nothing. Target the lowest common denominator.

We met once more, and the conversation was almost verbatim to the previous one. There was no progress whatsoever.

Mentoring takes commitment and progress from both parties. I wished them well in their pursuit.

# When to Refuse to Mentor Someone

*As a mentor, you have to be willing to put yourself in your mentee's shoes to understand the struggles that they deal with.*

—Toby Keith

Not every mentoring opportunity is destined to work, but there are circumstances where the mentorship should never even be considered. A resounding "no" is called for in a number of situations that, as a mentor, you just know are wrong, and fated to be thrown on the scrapheap. Just say NO.

- The desire and ambition of the mentee is just not there. Lacking these driving forces is a guarantee that the mentoring will be painfully slow, ineffective and one-sided.
- The mentee is ill-prepared, without a well-thought-out draft gameplan. This is typical of tire-kicker entrepreneurs.
- The basic entrepreneurial skillsets are not part of the mentee's toolbox. That makes the voyage far too demanding where mentoring starts at some sub zero level.
- Simply put, you are too busy to take on any more mentoring mandates. If you do, some mentorships will get short-changed.
- First two questions to ask the mentee are "What do you expect out of the mentoring process?" and "Why do you think your opportunity will succeed?" If these elicit a blank stare then it's time to set their goals, or to walk away. Maybe their dreams are still an empty canvas.
- Expectations regarding access to your time is another possible mentorship killer, especially after boundaries have been set. Mentees should not "own" you.
- If the mentee starts to ask questions that they could get from a Google or Edge or Safari search, that's a good reason to end it. Laziness is unacceptable. It also implies that the mentee is taking you for granted.
- It is assumed, and rightly so, that the mentor knows more than the mentee. The mentee needs to listen as much as they

speak. If the mentee is a "know-it-all," then mentoring is
unnecessary.

- "I've got a problem" needs to be business-related, not a plea
  for rent money or relationship counseling. If the mentee
  tries to broaden the association to include dealing with
  their personal relationships, it's time to reset the mentoring
  etiquette or call it a day.
- Sometimes there is an unexplainable bad chemistry between
  the mentor and mentee. You are uncomfortable. You will feel
  it almost instantly. Recommend another mentor.

# CHAPTER 5

# Corporate and Academic Mentoring Strategies

*Learning is finding out that you already know. Doing is demonstrating that you know it. Teaching is reminding others that they know just as well as you. You are all learners, doers, and teachers.*
—Richard Bach

## Corporate Mentorship Gameplanning

While mentoring is age-old, with deeply entrenched and proven models, there's always room for a new twist or three; innovative strategies designed to fit specific settings and circumstances.

### Peer-to-Peer Mentoring

Either within the corporate environment or one-on-one mentorship within the business or academic communities, it has been proven that some mentees prefer being mentored by someone at their same age group or level of business experience. Comfort and trust are key factors.

While this, at first glance, may have some drawbacks such as the depth of knowledge sharing, it is a model that works. The instant bonding established creates more of a team approach to mentoring. Each party learns from the other.

### Using Mentoring Software

Zoom, MSTeam, and other online forums have given birth to a new generation of mentoring, namely a host of software platforms that organize sessions, set agendas, supply teaching, and mentoring tools and resources.

track progress, collect feedback, send reminders, and facilitate connections by making the technology very user-friendly.

These tools also allow the participants to spend more time actually being involved in the mentorship journey and fewer headaches running, scheduling, recording, and sharing the results of the process.

Interested in finding out more? Try www.capterra.com/sem-compare/mentoring-software/ for an encapsulation of the highest-rated mentoring software platforms and their respective features.

### Reverse Mentoring

Younger mentors working with older mentees encourages knowledge sharing in the realm of technology, social media, and current business growth strategies. The ones with the know-how mentor the ones with experience/knowledge gaps, regardless of the disparity in their ages.

This is very prevalent in the corporate mentoring environment where new, young staff is engaged at a quick pace.

### Accountability Mentoring

This represents holding mentees accountable to make sure they do what they say they will do, and following through on action items mutually agreed to.

This type of mentoring gauges the seriousness of the participating mentee who, after several missed deliverables, can possibly be rejected from the mentoring journey.

### Boot Camp Mentoring

This represents the most stringent mentoring model whereby the mentor almost adopts the role of "chief inquisitor."

Tough questions are asked and the mentee is expected to be prepared or subsequently prepare responses that are big on facts and ideas and short on fluff.

As in "Accountability Mentoring" (above), there is a threat hanging over the mentorship that the journey can end if the mentee does not take this "hyper devil's advocate" approach seriously.

## Mentoring on the Fly

Quite often, unscheduled and spontaneous mentoring can yield surprisingly positive results. Ideas are shared and discussed when parties interact.

Google's Seattle, Washington's global engineering offices line its hallways with massive whiteboards for colleagues to meet spontaneously, share knowledge, and mentor new arrivals.

## Connection-Building Mentoring Model

Making connections is a critical component of succeeding in business, and is at the core of this mentoring model; knowledge sharing as it relates to business contacts and networking leads.

However this model also encompasses providing mentoring pertaining to the skills involved in networking and communications, two critical components of connection-building mentoring.

## Mentoring Within the Small Business

*Our chief want in life is somebody who will make us do what we can.*
—Ralph Waldo Emerson

Mentorship is a growing trend within corporations as mentoring programs are being developed and deployed to educate and share knowledge with employees and management, and build stronger teams within the corporate framework.

Mentorship programs, so prevalent in Fortune 500 companies, have now filtered down to small and medium businesses. The deliverables realized include the following:

- A stronger sense of loyalty and belonging from employees
- Key managers moving forward within the organizations as they are mentored to take on new roles and responsibilities
- Driving higher corporate culture adoption and engagement
- Meeting the workplace learning and development expectations of younger generations joining a company

- Knowledge sharing creates new opportunities for the business as mentoring opens new avenues for the team to follow through on ideas
- Corporate internal mentorship programs equate to greater satisfaction, less turnover, lower absenteeism, and reduced employee training costs
- Optimizing performance from employees and management
- Succession planning between older and younger staff

In a study conducted on the benefits of corporate culture, the results yielded the following observations:[1]

- Employee mentors within the company were promoted six times more often than those who did not take on mentoring roles.
- 25 percent of mentored staff received higher salaries. This represented a significant increase over non mentored team members.
- Mentees were promoted at an enhanced rate.
- The retention rate for mentored employees was significantly higher. More than 68 percent of mentors and mentees stayed with the company for five years or more.

Corporate-based mentorship programs have become a mainstay within companies. The knowledge sharing involves information and know-how related to the business, but also more generic personal development components.

The end result is the creation of a stronger and more resilient business run by a team of highly dedicated and confident staff and management.

**All of that having been said, the basic core mentoring program has not changed significantly as it is being delivered within a business environment.**

- It is still primarily one-on-one with goals and expectations set by both the mentor and the mentee.
- Sessions are held on a scheduled basis wherever feasible.

- The mentor acts as a sounding board for the mentee.
- Progress is tracked through the performance of the mentee.
- The mentorship has a finite lifespan and definable deliverables.

Simply put, mentoring and building a corporate mentorship culture is good for business.

## Business Mentoring in Academia

Academia is often cited as one of the birthplaces of mentorship. Many universities offer a business mentoring program that links academic programs with students interested in entrepreneurship as a career. The programs are intended to provide mentoring, provide business knowledge, and explore the realities of business beyond the classroom environment.

Business students get matched up with appropriate course mentors. The program generally starts with discussing the mentee's business ideas and gauging their commitment to entrepreneurship. Where interest is present, the mentoring model follows the traditional stages of interaction, exploring opportunities and building on the students' interests.

Further research has also yielded a host of mentoring models that are employed throughout universities, from "cluster mentoring" to creative matchups for participants to build closer relationships with their professors and creating greater resources for participating mentees.[*]

---

[*] See https://uen.pressbooks.pub/makingconnections/chapter/networked-mentoring-programs-in-academia/ "Networked Mentoring Programs in Academia." This highlights the full extent of informal and formal university-networked programs, structures, and mentoring models in academia.

# How Mentoring Has Changed

*If your actions inspire others to dream more, learn more, do more and become more, you are a leader.*

—John Quincy Adams

Over the years mentoring has changed because the very landscape of business has changed.

Technology has become a mainstay of the business environment; Google, Edge and Safari as search and research avenues; LinkedIn, Facebook, and Twitter for communications, GoFundMe and other crowdfunders for fundraising, and; various hyperactive social media platforms for marketing, branding, and customer loyalty generation. And it's all happened in the last several decades, or less.

Change in the very foundations of commerce has been dropped unceremoniously onto the businessperson in very short order. Fiercely competitive players all vying for the same marketplace have dumped this cacophony of technology onto the business world.

That's a simple observation, not an editorial commentary. It's just facts. **"Adapt or die" has become the rallying cry. The trends in mentoring have kept up with the times.**

*For the first time in recorded history, members from five different generations are working side-by-side in various industries. Traditionalists, or people born before 1946, hold seniority in the group, followed by the Baby Boomers, Generation X, Generation Y (Millennials), and Generation Z (Gen 2020).[†]*

The result is a mentoring phenomenon referred to as **"reverse mentoring."** A younger generation of successful businesspeople (and techies) is mentoring their peers, that is, the young are mentoring aging entrepreneurs

---

[†] https://medium.com/@KeithKrach/how-mentoring-has-changed-in-the-last-few-decades-1ca89bc9daf2

as well as older existing managers, teachers, trainers, and professors whose knowledge has been outpaced by the leaps in technology.

This applies equally to the **"mentoring of mentors**" as well, bringing established mentors into the twenty-first century.

This is particularly true in the corporate mentor-mentee framework where the "young guns" in the company work with the "older guard" in bringing them up to current business technology savvy (see the section titled "Mentoring Within the Small Business").

**The traditional model of the sage, older generation of mentors passing their wisdom onto mentees still exists, and is the established mainstay of mentorship.** However, with so many generations all active in the business milieu, relative youngsters are now also teaching an older generation who may be out of sync with today's resources and mentorship delivery platforms.

Changes have also been exacerbated by the delivery vehicles now so prevalent.

- Zoom became a household personal communications tool in the time of Covid and remains the world's number one online vehicle for mentoring and training.
- Webinar platforms including, but not limited to ClickMeeting, GoToWebinar, and Zoom, Microsoft Meetings, amongst others, all vie for attention in a very crowded marketplace.[‡]

The implication is that mentorship using these vehicles has adapted in terms of delivery style, personal interaction, and content sharing.

In my own mentoring experience, the demand among mentees has always prioritized business planning, marketing, and fundraising. However, technology and social media have now made their way to the top five list of "asks."

Another factor in the mentoring landscape is the growth of women in business. Women have become leaders in online training, coaching, and one-on-one mentoring, capitalizing on their presence in business as well

---

[‡] www.forbes.com/advisor/business/software/best-webinar-software/

as their rapid uptake in the use of online delivery platforms. It is timely, and it is highly effective.

There has also been a marked increase in fees-for-services business mentoring, as witnessed by multi million "hits" that Mr. Google offers up in a split second of market research. This sector is now more pronounced than ever.

Finally, mentoring has become very "sector-specific." Mentors are packaging themselves as experts in two ways: (1) by their experience and knowledge base in technology, resources, retail, health care, transportation, or any other distinct sector venues that reflect their background, and (2) by their skillsets, namely mergers and acquisitions, marketing, finance and investment, human resources, business planning, and so on.

This is reflected in the fact that mentees are now often working with a team of mentor specialists as opposed to a mentor generalist.

All of that having been said, **the very core fundamentals of mentoring have not changed**. The interpersonal skillsets demand more effective communications across a host of new delivery venues paralleling traditional mentoring avenues and knowledge-sharing priorities.

Most importantly, **the need for mentoring is ever-present and growing**, particularly as competition in the business environment makes it tougher on newbie entrepreneurs to fight for a foothold and gain market penetration.

# CHAPTER 6

# Mentoring as a Fees-for-Services Business

*We make a living by what we get, but we make a life by what we give.*

—Winston Churchill

## The Fee-Based Mentor

In the context of this book, mentoring is generally associated with a core of seasoned businesspeople volunteering their time to share their experiences and knowledge base with a new generation of entrepreneurs. That is the tradition of mentorship provided through academic universities' business programs, foundations, and government agencies that foster entrepreneurial development.

However, business mentoring is also a quasi-profession, where private consultants, accountants, and management consultants, among others, mentor on a fees-for-services basis.

There is a debate that believes "mentoring" is free and "business coaching" is delivered on a fees-for-services basis. Frankly, the distinction between these two practices/occupations/vocations is fuzzy at best. In practical terms, they are the same, but coaching is better defined as revenue-generating mentoring activities such as workshops, webinars, creating resource materials (such as this book), and other "for profit" avenues.

Hence, paid mentoring is "coaching," and free coaching is "mentoring." The differences are ambiguous.

In fact, virtually every Business Consultant is, to some degree, a mentor, working with clients on their projects, and helping companies and entrepreneurs realize on their business plans, and tackle problems and contentious issues.

To that end, only a limited discussion of mentoring for fees is a worthwhile exercise.

After thirty years of professional mentoring as a Business Consultant (as well as untold volunteer mentoring hours), I have compiled advice best characterized as "**mentoring advice for the professional remunerated mentor.**"

The following is based solely on my own experience. However, rest assured, the advice being shared below works, as proven by the reasonable success of my multi location business consulting practice, staffed by an army of bright, overpaid young consultants. Our group was mandated to assist with hundreds of millions of dollars of client projects around the globe. Call it what you will, but it was mentoring.

Here is some food-for-thought for established fee-for-service mentoring/coaching consultants as well as those thinking of taking up the career challenge.

First and foremost, **create revenue-generating profit centers**. There are numerous. Select the ones you are most comfortable developing and delivering.

- Webinars
- Workshops
- Online mentoring sessions
- Resource handbooks and other material
- Digital "for pay" workshops and sessions dealing with various aspects of entrepreneurship
- Contracting with universities and training institutes, including university-level workshops
- Helping to develop Mentoring Plans
- Corporate and professional mentoring programs

You are selling an intangible. If the client is unhappy with you, as sometimes happens (but shouldn't), the consultant has little recourse. The advice is **to get partial (or all) payment up front**. Sadly, in disputes, the consultant needs the upper hand for leverage.

Mentors are usually older, (supposedly) wiser, and more experienced than those being mentored. Fees should reflect your expertise gleaned from a number of years in business, and working with other businesses, academia, and entrepreneurs.

On the assumption that you cannot do everything yourself, it is best to build a **virtual team of sub contracted consultants**, each with their own areas of expertise (technology, marketing, money, business planning, etc.). In this way your business can be seen as a "full-service house," and each subcontractor's services would be marked up for profit.

**Hiring consultants** (preferably as contractors) is always a challenge. My technique was to present candidates with a business mentoring scenario and ask how they would structure a Mentoring Plan. The good candidates often showed amazing creativity and imagination. The weak (and/or lazy) candidates fell by the wayside. The distinction between the two groups was razor-sharp.

**Non disclosure Agreements** with your people are important. While these NDAs have more impact as moral bludgeons than legal safeguards, they will give any contractor or employee second thoughts about walking away with your Intellectual Property and client base.

You likely cannot be a mentor to everyone in every sector. **Choose your target market group** within a workable geographic zone and concentrate your efforts there. For example, it's better to be known as the "experts in technology" than "those guys who think they know everything about everything."

The better you build your reputation, the easier it will be to market, especially when clients search you out. Until then, there are a number of **marketing avenues I have used successfully**, and am pleased to share these with you.

- Networking everywhere, continuously, at events, conferences, parties, "the club," gatherings and specifically designed networking sessions
- Speaking engagements
- Writing articles in trade magazines and journals that reach your target market group(s)
- Free editorials written about your clients
- Branding your business around something memorable, generally a client's success story that moves people

- Coattailing on the marketing initiatives with related but non-competitive companies
- Anywhere and everywhere your prospective clients see your name

We live in a litigious world, and when you are doling out advice, you are exposing yourself to the possibility of legal repercussions from disgruntled clients. Protect yourself with **liability insurance to cover any eventualities**. Many of the larger organizations, universities, and corporations will demand proof of your liability insurance.

All proposals, bids, and invoices should have reference to you delivering these services "on a **best efforts basis**."

As well, your **client expectations** need to be spelled out before you undertake a mission. Otherwise, the list of your expected services can be never-ending.

The **best clients to pursue are "annuity based"** where your mentoring is delivered over a number of months (or even years), and you are paid a monthly retainer. If you succeed in servicing a number of these retainer-based contracts, your cash flow will thank you.

One lesser-used twist when discussing fee structures, particularly with new or young businesses, is taking your **fees in shares in your client's enterprise**. Obviously, this will depend on your own consulting business's strength, and your ability to roll the dice on something you think will have significant payback, but risky in the client's formative years. Weight the present versus the "maybe" future rewards. Remember that, once you have completed your work for the client, they are on their own. You have little control as to whether they score, or simply fade away into business oblivion. If you take shares, try to stay involved on their Board.

In one case, I had a client whose founders were brilliant techs. They were involved in ground-breaking advanced 3D animation. As exciting as that sounded, they were financial paupers. I was offered a share of their business and technology IP ownership. I graciously declined.

The company went on to work on The Terminator series and Star Wars, and was bought by Lucasfilm for a veritable fortune.

The marginal fees I actually collected from them? Long spent and a very distant memory.

# More Mentorship Tools and Lessons

*The greatest good you can do for another does not just share your riches but to reveal to him his own.*

—Benjamin Disraeli

## Experience Is a Great Teacher

No book of mine is complete with a rendition of yet more stories. For the reader, each story ends with a (hopefully) valuable learning experience.

For me, recounting these adventures and misadventures is a stroll through memory lane. With several decades to draw on, the memories run deep.

### The Author's Own Mentoring World

In retrospect, I have been mentored and enjoyed mentoring for the better part of my work life.

From my first job in charge of accounts receivable for six divisions of a clothing manufacturer where I was taught "Here's how to collect tough accounts without strong-arming or threatening to hand the file over to Constantine." to Group Controller for twenty-six diverse operations within a major multinational.

This required 'Cirque du Soleil' style juggling skills, micromanaging, tightrope acrobatics and delegating responsibilities.

My business adventures culminated in my starting and spearheading the growth of my own Business Consulting Firm, with a team of thirty-five, prima-donna-like consultants who helped me define the term "mentoring."

Of course, as with any start-up junkie, my entrepreneurial pathway was sprinkled with shiny coins along the way. Glistening coins that I could not pass by as I flirted with other business opportunities.

With each new business I started, or opportunities I undertook, I sought out mentors who could offer real-world advice, ideas, and, of course, tried to heed warnings about my endeavors, especially where I might have discounted the risks, and been blinded by potential returns.

These were different mentors in my network, sporting dissimilar experience and expertise.

- Role models running similar or complimentary companies
- Learning to maintain a carefree, confident, and de-stressed environment
- Elastic ethics to skate and charm through any situation, including closing contract sales and building a network of contacts (and fans)
- Strategic planning and forward-thinking business development
- The art of networking and "hot button pushing" to get the results I sought
- Communications, and the psychology of business to capitalize on contacts as steppingstones to collect greater shiny coins

**The point is to seek out mentors who are useful to you, in specific circumstances, and who fill different needs. There are few "one-size-fits-all" mentors who can deliver everything effectively.**

### Old Dogs, New Tricks

At my consulting firm, I was surrounded by a small army consisting of young, well-educated employees, many far better versed than I in areas of technology, who were innovating and reshaping business almost daily.

My objective was to get each person to think like an entrepreneur and bring any ideas and proposed initiatives to me for discussion. There were rewards set for implementable gems.

While my experience was based on mentoring the fundamentals of business, my team became my window to the changing marketplace, especially from a technology viewpoint.

Unknowingly, this was "Reverse Mentoring" as it is known today. However, back then, it was simply a logical response to staying competitive, technology-friendly, and alert to new opportunities for growth.

My team learned almost as much from me as I learned from them.

Over the course of this reverse mentoring, the company was actually reborn on several occasions, and far more receptive to meeting client and marketplace needs.

### Bad Partners Incapable of Being Mentored

There were two occasions where mentoring turned out to be a lost cause.

**Partner A**, let's call him Johnny-One Note, had only one arrogant style of communicating with people. In networking situations, mixing with other narcissistic souls, he was marvelous. A true natural.

However, he terrified employees and talked down to many clients, not realizing that his pomposity was not always an asset, but a weapon.

I tried to limit his exposure to being out in the business world where he was among his equals. It was an ecosphere I detested mingling in. I took over mentoring our team of consultants. To their relief, my style was far more "humane." It worked.

It was a case of "making do," and properly matching up the mentor and mentees.

**Communication style is a big part of mentoring. It can reinforce or destroy the process.**

**Partner B** came into the business with some valuable assets, but also one major deficit, which was an inability or willingness to listen. In dealing with clients, he would propose what he felt they needed and often not what they wanted.

For example, he once proposed that we carry out an overpriced $245,000 Marketing Strategy for a cash-strapped client who had turned to us to find an investor. Incompatibility is often based on foolhardy over-confidence and arrogance.

Partner B reminded me of the tagline for the now-defunct Coconut Joe Clothing Company—*A Legend in His Own Mind*.

Mentoring was pointless, despite several efforts to initiate some discourse. Training my hamster was easier.

**The lesson here is that if you assess the mentor as decidedly difficult, stubborn, or immovable, then walk away. Quickly.**

## Age Mellows

I was blessed with a business friend who, in his youth, was reputed to be a bulldog in business. His decisions dictated the company's direction. Discussion was for hippies. Management by committee garnered a "no" before it could even be seriously considered.

He was a team player with no teammates.

At one point, in the midst of a negotiation with an important Asian supplier who was deemed of questionable virtue but was also a critical part of his supply chain, my friend quietly informed the supplier's negotiator that he would suffer painful personal physical consequences should any shipment be short-changed or arrive sporting inferior product quality.

Such was my friend the bulldog. Fun, engaging, but slightly unhinged.

Then aging found him. He mellowed. He started showing an interest in the knowledge base that surrounded him in his business, and opened himself up to being mentored by his more youthful compatriots.

The next step, which surprised me, is that he took up mentoring others, transferring the knowledge and business acumen that had made him so successful, but mercifully toned down somewhat.

**Age provides the ability to experience, try, fail, and relearn. As such, many mentors are retirees or close to retiring, but have put in the time to learn to succeed in business. It's called "wisdom."**

**Don't sell any older mentor short. Picture them as bulldogs in their formative years.**

## Crypto King No More

Ever known someone who claimed amassing great wealth playing the crypto game? This is usually interspersed with losing everything, then flirting with wealth again, and so the yo-yo yo-yos.

My mentee client was an astute businessperson whose one terrible habit was crypto distraction, which, I assumed, was a gambling addiction. He would constantly extol the "huge" profits (and very few losses, strangely enough) he had made each day trading in the crypto shark pool.

The issues that came up in the mentoring process were a lack of focus, research, and homework for his own project not done, and a fierce case of distraction.

We set timelines. They went by the wayside. We identified risks, and they were glossed over. And so, it took the downhill slide until I called for an end to the mentoring exercise, and an offer to pick it up again when he had lost enough money to put an end to his crypto trading.

He did, and we fulfilled his mentoring journey together.

**Distraction in the mentoring process is destructive. Call your mentee on it, fix it, or find mentees who are more ready to actively participate, and listen.**


### The Chameleon

Dusty was an ambitious and reasonably talented entrepreneur. Her experience was best described as "dabbling," trying new ventures, many of which were clearly quick-in-quick-out fads. For each of her initiatives she was enthusiastically all in, then refocused on the next shiny coin on the road, then the next, and on it went.

In our mentoring, I tried to convey to her the concept of prioritizing her goals and aspirations, and identifying which of her business ideas would deliver the results she sought with the least resistance or roadblocks.

What I realized after several sessions that it was the "chase" that excited her. Not running the business. No long-term plans. Few details other than the thrill of the possibilities.

Interestingly enough, I empathized with her. We shared stories. We start-up junkies need to stick together.

I, personally, had matured past the kind of rashness and instant gratification that was enveloping Dusty, but I remembered it well.

I jokingly told her to contact me once she decided what she wanted to do when she grew up. She actually did.

**Before you take on any mentees, make sure they are ready to take on the responsibilities associated with being a mentee. There are**

expectations; checklists and self-assessment readiness tests in this book, as well as mentorship boundaries, mutual expectations, and goal-setting exercises. Get familiar with them.

### No! No! Well, Maybe, Yes!

My client had created an innovative line of facial and skin creams composed entirely of natural healing ingredients. This was a well-received product line and a hit at craft markets.

I was engaged to mentor and work with her to rebrand, since the packaging and labeling was quite homemade-looking. This was in preparation for developing a new vendor network to cover fourteen cities. It was an exciting proposition.

The problem was that every idea I brought to the table yielded a resounding "NO." Even ideas she herself generated eventually met the same fate after some brainstorming.

I came to the realization that she simply did not want to change anything. Perhaps it was a fear of change, or "if it ain't broke, don't fix it." The product and packaging simply wouldn't work in the selected upscale markets. There was a distinct "conflict of will" working here.

I approached her and asked her two simple questions; (1) "Do you trust me?" and (2) "You hired me to work with you, mentor and kick new ideas around. If everything we create together is "NO," why did you even hire me?"

Silence ensued. The reality of our head-butting mentoring became clear to her, and she ceded some control to me.

The new campaign was built on the strengths of her existing foundation. The expansion was a success. The client was thrilled, as was I.

**Trust is a major component of mentoring. Without it, the process is a non starter. Work to build trust right from the get-go.**

### Duking It Out

Two friends went into business together as partners. They both had a background in their chosen field. My role was to mentor the two, together, help build a cohesive team, and guide them through the planning and launch of their venture.

Very shortly into the mentorship, I realized that they mistrusted each other. They argued incessantly. Black and white. Day and night. It was tiresome.

I called a halt to the sessions, and confronted them, asking why, if they fought each other (and me) at every move, did they ever decide to go into business together? There was an illogic working here.

It turned out that they were notoriously competitive, and this proposed business venture was a game in which each fought to be the Alpha dog.

The only way this could be saved was getting agreement on what they wanted in the venture, what specific steps would get them there, and what each could contribute. Nothing else. Everything else was to be left at the door.

With this narrow focus on the mentoring mandate, everything fell into place. I ended the mentoring journey as soon as the goals were achieved and there was peaceful coexistence between them.

Did it last? Not sure. I was leery to jostle the beast.

**Lesson learned. When more than one mentee is involved in the process, first determine that they are prepared to act as one, and not as combatants. More importantly, set clearly defined expectations as to what each player is bringing to the table.**

### Bow Before the Gatekeeper

My mentoring client had created a software application similar to what Square D and others offered retailers. It was innovative in design and offered increased benefits to the host and the customer.

Here was a case of a great product with no home. The industry was "owned" by major banks. Any and all inroads attempted were either ignored or rebuffed before my client could present their PowerPoint Deck and financial model.

That was the challenge. We spent a number of sessions discussing possibilities. I offered up two potential solutions drawn from my own experiences in dealing with the aloof "Old Boys Club."

- To get to the decision makers you need to get past their gatekeepers. These Executive Assistant gatekeepers screened what landed on the right people's desks. Befriend the gatekeepers and you can gain access to those who could accept the merits of their application, and hopefully agree to a beta test. That was their goal.
- In some instances, my client was uncertain what level of executive to approach. I suggested that anyone with a title like Chief Technology Officer or Strategic Business Development and Acquisitions would be appropriate.
  - Where to find the contact names? Most target audience companies were publicly traded and produced Annual Reports with all the names and information my client sought. If necessary, I suggested they may need to buy a single share in the company to get a copy of the Report.

**Where the mentoring process includes creative dialog between mentor and mentee, and the mentor can share knowledge and experience, then mentorship can work, as it did in this case.**

### Tell Me What You Do?

This is a question I often ask at the beginning of mentorship, or even during the prescreening phase. Logic would dictate that the mentee knows what they do and where they are heading. Wrong. Not always so.

In one instance, my task was to mentor a social organization's leadership in order to prepare them to meet new funders.

The organization delivered a number of programs, mostly unrelated to each other, and none worthy of a stand-alone presence. So, when I asked, they fumbled. No elevator pitches. Nothing substantial that the funder could easily get their arms around.

The other issue was that they lived on grants. Small handouts, actually, that kept them living a "hand-to-mouth" subsistence. They deserved far better.

Mentoring a social organization in the ways of business is difficult. This was a different world for them.

However, diligently, we prioritized their services and helped develop a transition plan for revenue generation emanating from their program offerings.

They were the ideal mentees; eager, bright, committed to change. It all worked.

**When the client has specific and identified needs and a commitment and focus to participate in mentorship, even the tough challenges can be conquered.**

### Slow Down and Think Baby Steps

My client was in the investment counseling business, and had just partnered with an insurance company that offered an innovative tax avoidance arrangement. It was entirely legal, but pretty involved and complex.

I knew my client was being coached by the insurance people so as to be able to present the pros and cons of the scheme in the form of a "what if" PowerPoint Deck which walked any potential participant/investor through the maze.

My mentee client asked if he could practice on me, and I readily agreed. I thought that I might be the ideal beta test since my knowledge of insurance and detailed investment scenarios was scanty.

As he launched into his presentation (and annoyingly spelling my name wrong in the investment charts) it became clear that I was lost right after "Hi Jay."

I did manage to ask some semi-intelligent questions, many of which he stumbled through with semi-acceptable answers. My feeling was that if I could stump him, anyone could.

It was pretty obvious that he knew far more than me, assumed I knew as much as he did, and was in a hurry to sign me up. Overzealous was an understatement of his style, even though I was still hovering around "Hi Jay," as I mentioned.

**The lesson here was conveying the virtue of "baby steps," going slowly and dealing with each fragment, each molecule of a presentation or pitch in sufficient detail that all parties were comfortable moving on.**

### I Was "Used and Abused"

The scenario involved a group that delivered "feel good" programs and services, from wellness training and meditational healing, to social and sensitivity awareness.

The challenge was that they hovered between a social entity and a business trying to survive, and their business model was pitifully weak.

The mentoring sessions proceeded on track. The feedback from the group was excellent. I felt strongly that we were on track to make a difference for them.

Unfortunately, they never seemed to follow through on most of the action items we mutually agreed upon for them to pursue. Coupled with a multitude of missed or rebooked meetings, progress slowed down to a snail's pace. My curiosity twitched.

I discovered that the mentorship was really a prerequisite recommended by an existing funder before they would complete a new funding program.

There was no interest in the mentoring itself other than providing lip service to the funder. I was being used.

Had they informed me of the purpose of the mentoring program, I would have understood. However, hiding the funders' intent was a mistake.

When the funder asked me for a progress report, I simply replied "few discernable results."

**One of the foundations of mentoring is transparency, and when that does not materialize, then the process of mentorship cannot survive for very long.**

### When Mentoring Touches Your Heart

The client was a mega-talented First Nations (native) artist whose life story was fraught with a history of foster homes, family violence, and poverty. The end result was that she was withdrawn and introverted, but expressed herself through her art.

She struggled financially.

While she was open to mentoring, her insecurities dampened her ability to fully participate. I had to change my tactics.

Instead of focusing on the business elements of entrepreneurship, I spent time building trust and open communication. It was an ordeal of tiny but progressive steps. Only once we had achieved a semblance of trust, entrepreneurship mentoring followed.

At the end of our journey, she had several exhibits at influential art galleries and even had two paintings in a national museum.

For years, one of her paintings graced my office, with a warm note of thanks inscribed on the back. It made me glow with contentment.

**Sometimes, in rare circumstances, the mentor needs to backtrack and start the process with developing an interpersonal relationship and trust. Once achieved, success should follow. It's worth the effort.**

### More Real-Life Mentorship Journeys

*Mentoring is a brain to pick, an ear to listen, and a push in the right direction.*

—John Crosby

Not every mentoring experience is a winner. While some are great, others are mediocre; a small handful have pointless go-nowhere outcomes. However, the ones that work are life-changing for the mentees, and extremely rewarding for the mentor. Imagine how these "aha moments of appreciation" can and do galvanize your desire to mentor.

Here are a few excerpts from letters of appreciation received from several of the author's mentees. They are all reprinted with permission from the writers.

*I wanted to take a moment to express how truly grateful I am for your mentoring. It has made a remarkable impact on my journey as an entrepreneur. The opportunity to be able to turn ideas into solid plans with guidance is simply incredible.*

*A couple of years ago, I attended a business webinar led by you, and it was a game-changer for me. The insights I gained were like opening a new window, expanding my understanding, and sparking a real passion for learning and growing. Little did I know, this would be a life-changing decision. I can't thank you enough for the chance to work with you.*

*As someone who's always bubbling with ideas, I often found myself lost in a sea of possibilities. I'd get caught up in planning, but struggle to move forward. This mentoring has been my guiding light, helping me face my fears and steering me toward success. Your support and honest advice have been crucial in shaping my journey. I can't put into words how thankful I am.*

*I'm excited about all the aspiring entrepreneurs who will benefit from your mentoring advice in the future. Your support will undoubtedly touch many lives, just as it has touched mine.*

—Monicque K.

*I am writing to express my sincere appreciation for the immense coaching and business development support I received as a direct result from you as both mentor and coach in my recent business development and enhancement efforts.*

*It is extremely rewarding to engage in a process, which was confusing and filled with obstacles at the outset; then to have the support and direction of mentorship, that is both experienced and efficient, to walk me through the process of evaluations, options, focus, and specific targets. These were some of the great benefits I experienced in your mentoring. Thank you Sincerely.*

*Also, the present momentum which I have consequently been able to engage is a total game changer for my business career. Your coaching has been invaluable in the complete turnaround and success of my business.*

—Ted D., Integrity Solutions

Letters like this are the inspiration that drives mentors to do even more with each new mentee relationship.

# APPENDIX 1

# Mentoring Video Resources

## Learn From Other Experts

Sometimes learning or fine-tuning a skill is best accomplished with visual tools. As such, I have compiled a number of valuable YouTube videos on the benefits, techniques, and 'artform' of mentoring, for mentors and mentees.[1]

Ten Best TED Talks on Mentorship
www.growthmentor.com/blog/ted-talks-on-mentorship/

What is Mentoring?
www.youtube.com/watch?v=yqaS7jOA1b8

How to Be a Good Mentor
www.ted.com/playlists/400/how_to_be_a_good_mentor

Mentoring Works! Collection (Links) of Excellent Short Videos on Mentoring
http://mentoring-works.com/resources/videos/

Kenneth Ortiz: How to Be a Great Mentor (TED Talks)
www.ted.com/talks/kenneth_ortiz_how_to_be_a_great_mentor

---

[1] It should be noted that these video links are listed herein strictly as examples. They are not paid sponsors and not recommended as the sole providers the reader should research.

Mastering Mentoring (Video)
www.mindtools.com/aici9yf/mastering-mentoring-video

Tools for Mentors and Mentees
www.mentoringpartnership.ca/mentoring-tools/

Why the Power of Mentoring Can Change the World
www.youtube.com/watch?v=u4kTlK5mUHc

Mentoring Is Inspirational
www.youtube.com/watch?v=kFSaguaHGzg

Inspirational Mentor Theme Movie Clips for Teaching
www.wingclips.com/themes/mentor

The Power of Mentoring Programs
www.chieflearningofficer.com/2023/07/21/video-the-power-of-
mentoring-programs/

# APPENDIX 2

# More Mentoring Resources and Learning Opportunities

How does the mentor build a personal inventory of business wealth and acumen to pass along to mentees? Certainly, by years of experience which morphs into wisdom. This explains why so many volunteer mentors are retired businesspeople with the knowledge base and time availability to get involved.

But there are many other opportunities to advance and fine-tune your mentoring skills and techniques.

**Role Models**—Find other mentors whose style is compatible with yours, and shadow them. Mentor with them. Learn from their delivery and ability to gain the trust and confidence of their mentees and, consequently, deliver results. Role modeling is my highest recommended technique.

**Mentoring Associations**—They abound. There are national, international, regional, community-based, clubs, industry-based, and academia-based mentoring associations worth researching. Carefully review their programs, as a number of them are fees-for-services private consulting companies posing as associations. Do your homework carefully.

**Conferences**—Each presents the opportunity to network, build a contacts portfolio, and possibly even identify others with whom you can jointly offer mentoring programs.

**Academic Programs**—Many universities and colleges offer mentoring courses, diplomas, and certifications. They are generally couched in business management or leadership degrees. There is also a database of universities (and their weblinks) that offer programs in leadership skills, human resources, and other skillsets. One such example

worth exploring is www.coursera.org/courses?query=mentoring).[*]
There are others you may wish to investigate as well.

**Online Mentoring Software and Courses**—For those interested
in online courses, there are a number worth looking into. One
such online delivery platform is 'together' located at ww.together-
platform.com/blog/online-mentoring-courses.[†]

**Foundations**—There are mentoring foundations generally associated
with universities. Their role revolves around the aspects of mentoring, generally as a function of teaching in an academic environment.

---

[*] It should be noted that these websites and providers are listed herein strictly as
examples. They are not paid sponsors and not recommended as the sole providers
the reader should research.

[†] Ibid.

# Notes

## Chapter 1

1. Silverberg (2020); Silverberg and McLean (2021); Silverberg (February 2023); Silverberg (December 2023).
2. Workplace Loyalties Change, but the Value of Mentoring Doesn't (n.d.).

## Chapter 5

1. Workplace Loyalties Change, but the Value of Mentoring Doesn't (n.d.).

# References

Silverberg, J.J. October 2020. *A Business Cynic's Wisdom: Winning Through Flexible Ethics*. Business Expert Press.

Silverberg, J.J. and B.E McLean. November 2021. *Dead Fish Don't Swim Upstream: Real Life Lessons in Entrepreneurship*. Business Expert Press.

Silverberg, J.J February 2023. *Stuck Entrepreneurs: Escape Routes Out of the Quicksand.* Business Expert Press.

Silverberg, J.J. December 2023. *The Start-Up Junkie's Playbook: A 30 Step Plan to Launch Your Business*. Business Expert Press. www.businessexpertpress.com/jay-j-silverberg/

*Workplace Loyalties Change, but the Value of Mentoring Doesn't.* n.d. Wharton School, University of Pennsylvania. https://knowledge.wharton.upenn.edu/podcast/knowledge-at-wharton-podcast/workplace-loyalties-change-but-the-value-of-mentoring-doesnt/

Ibid.

# About the Author

**Jay J. Silverberg** is a "business rebel" who has started and run a number of successful businesses. This book is based on his **business mentoring experience and adventures (and misadventures)** and offers up a multitude of inestimably valuable lessons. As an entrepreneurial trainer, Jay has developed innovative programs for both the beginner and the advanced businessperson and delivered training and mentoring to thousands of entrepreneurs, managers, and business professionals.

As a business consultant, Jay's practice ranged from start-ups to Fortune 500 firms with projects that have spanned the globe. He has also represented government trade and economic development ministries at national and international conferences.

Jay currently teaches various levels of entrepreneurship and delivers business consulting, coaching, and mentoring.

Jay resides in Vancouver, British Columbia, Canada, with his wife, Linda, who inspires him to always see life as a gift and business as a game (and vice versa). Jay can be contacted at silverberg88@gmail.com.

## Related Books

Silverberg, J.J. October 2020. *A Business Cynic's Wisdom: Winning Through Flexible Ethics*. Business Expert Press.

Silverberg, J.J. and B.E. McLean. November 2021. *Dead Fish Don't Swim Upstream: Real Life Lessons in Entrepreneurship*. Business Expert Press.

Silverberg, J.J. February 2023. *Stuck Entrepreneurs: Escape Routes Out of the Quicksand*. Business Expert Press.

Silverberg, J.J. December 2023. *The Start-Up Junkie's Playbook: A 30-Step Plan to Launch Your Business*. Business Expert Press.

# Index

## OTHER TITLES IN THE ENTREPRENEURSHIP AND SMALL BUSINESS MANAGEMENT COLLECTION

Scott Shane, Case Western University, Editor

- *So You Want to Start a Business* by John B. Vinturella
- *Spinout Ventures* by Andre Laplume and Sepideh Yeganegi
- *Unleashing the Startup Unicorn* by Vivek Kale
- *The Start-Up Junkie's Playbook* by Jay J. Silverberg
- *The Most Common Entrepreneurial Mistakes and How to Avoid Them* by Lisa MacDonald
- *The Hybrid Entrepreneur* by Kevin Scanlon
- *Stuck Entrepreneurs* by Jay Silverberg
- *Teaching Old Dogs New Tricks* by Thomas Waters
- *Building Business Capacity* by Sheryl Hardin
- *The Entrepreneurial Adventure* by Oliver James
- *So, You Bought a Franchise. Now What?* by David Roemer
- *The Startup Masterplan* by Nikhil Agarwal and Krishiv Agarwal
- *Managing Health and Safety in a Small Business* by Jacqueline Jeynes
- *Modern Devil's Advocacy* by Robert Koshinskie

# Concise and Applied Business Books

The Collection listed above is one of 30 business subject collections that Business Expert Press has grown to make BEP a premiere publisher of print and digital books. Our concise and applied books are for...

- Professionals and Practitioners
- Faculty who adopt our books for courses
- Librarians who know that BEP's Digital Libraries are a unique way to offer students ebooks to download, not restricted with any digital rights management
- Executive Training Course Leaders
- Business Seminar Organizers

Business Expert Press books are for anyone who needs to dig deeper on business ideas, goals, and solutions to everyday problems. Whether one print book, one ebook, or buying a digital library of 110 ebooks, we remain the affordable and smart way to be business smart. For more information, please visit www.businessexpertpress.com, or contact sales@businessexpertpress.com.

www.ingramcontent.com/pod-product-compliance
Lightning Source LLC
Chambersburg PA
CBHW061321220326
41599CB00026B/4982